# MAD CLOT ON A HOLY BONE

# MAD CLOT ON A HOLY BONE

**MEMORIES OF A PSYCHIC THEATER**

With Contributions by
Mark Allen, Tim Reid,
Janet Sarbanes,
and Lucas Wrench

Edited by Mark Allen
and Deirdre O'Dwyer

Asher Hartman

Designed by Becca Lofchie
Edited by Mark Allen and Deirdre O'Dwyer
Project management by Addy Rabinovitch
Illustrations by Tiffanie Tran
Proofread by Olivia Weber-Stenis
Color separations by Echelon, Santa Monica, California
Printed and bound by Cantz, Esslingen, Germany

Photography credits are provided on pages 168–69.

First edition of 1500

Typeset in Galaxie Copernicus and Galaxie Polaris and printed on Munken Lynx Rough and Magno Satin papers.



Cover: Performance view, *Purple Electric Play (PEP!)*, Machine Project, Los Angeles, 2014; Star (Philip Littell). Photo by Marianne Williams, Courtesy Gawdafful National Theater

Library of Congress Cataloguing-in-Publication Data is available upon request.

ISBN 978-0-9988616-7-8

**X ARTISTS' BOOKS**

X Artists' Books
PO Box 3424
South Pasadena, CA 91031
USA
www.xartistsbooks.com

# Contents

Asher Hartman dedicates this
book to Mark Allen, Candice Lin, and
in memory of Haruko Tanaka

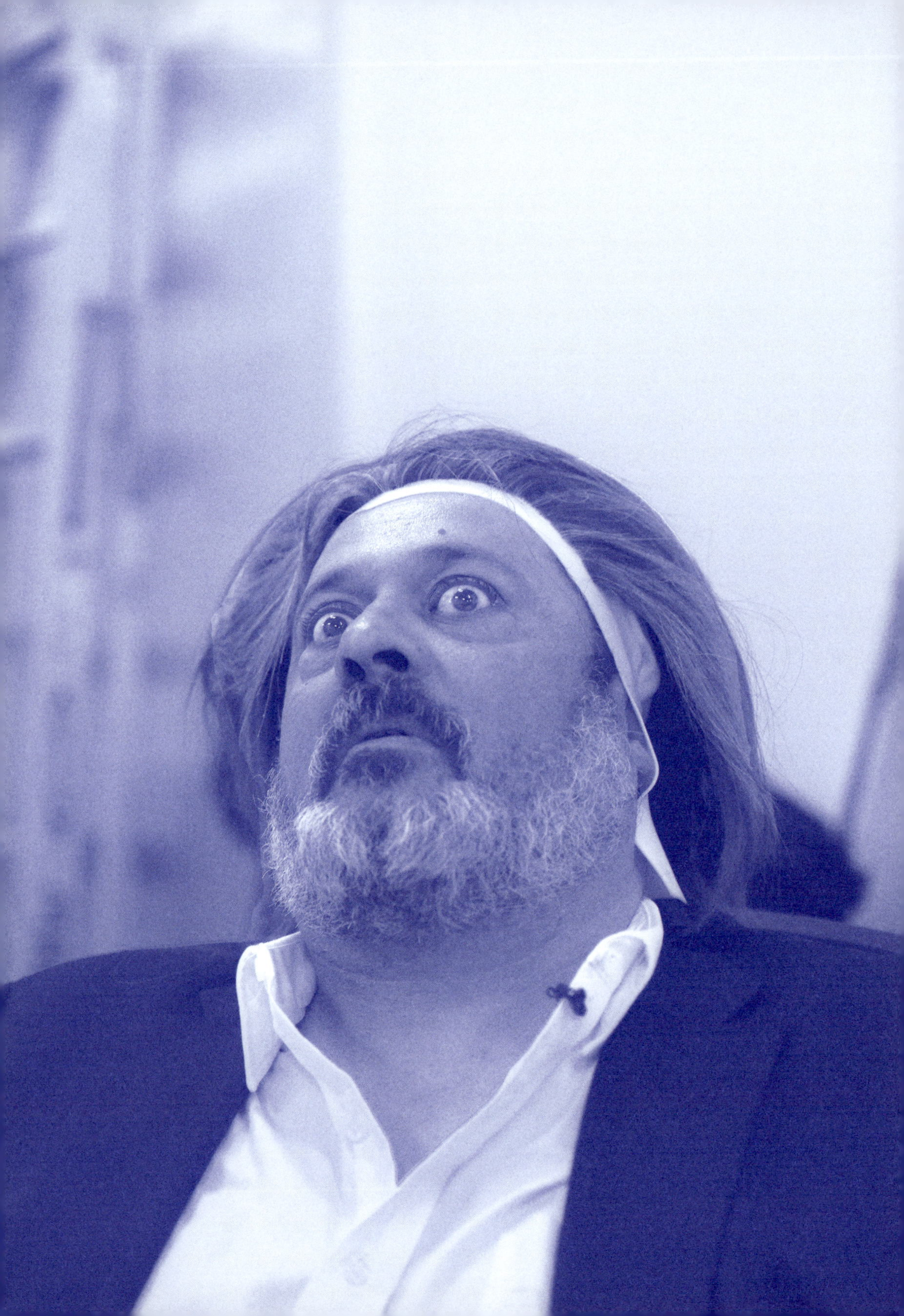

# MAD CLOT ON A HOLY BONE

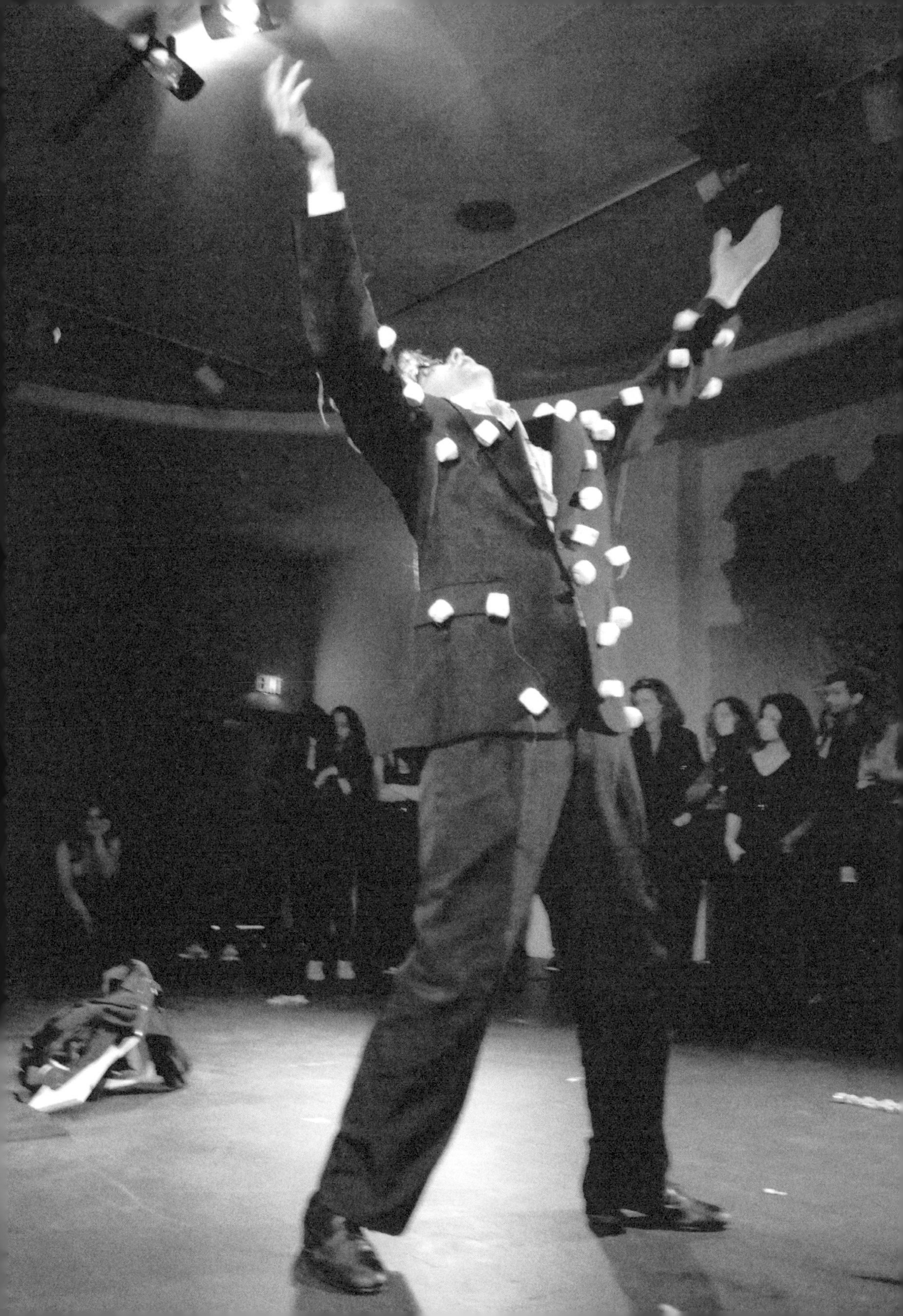

# The Gawdafful Plays of Asher Hartman

Janet Sarbanes

Upon walking into my first Asher Hartman play, *See What Love the Father Has Given Us* (2012), I was guided down a dark hallway by a kind and glamorous drag queen (Marcus Kuiland-Nazario) and into a facsimile of the break room at a big box store, where, after offering us a taste of whisky, Joe Seely and Jasmine Orpilla launched into a mating dance of biblical proportions. We were seated no more than a foot away from the actors, and I spent the first few minutes of the performance in a panic that I might be asked to participate. But it quickly became apparent that this was not that kind of play. The Gawdafful National Theater held me close, but not that close. As Hartman describes it, I was acknowledged as an audience member, not a participant—a nod he frequently makes to the structural antagonism that always exists between actors and audience (those unspoken questions: "Why are you looking at me? Why am I having to look at you?").

This attention to the frame is a constant feature of Hartman's work, which includes nine productions to date. Early plays push the boundaries of various performance genres, as in *The All Stars of Non Violet Communication* (2011), which probes the conventions of stand-up comedy, exposing their violence, and *Annie Okay* (2010), which explores the "colonialist subtext in two of America's most beloved musicals, *Annie Get Your Gun* and *The King and I*."[1] Later works such as *Purple Electric Play (PEP!)* (2014) and *Mr. Akita* (2015) take on the histories and practices of theater and painting. But while making us conscious of the traditions they're working in, the challenge these plays pose is existential rather than cerebral: The frame—whatever it may be—simply cannot contain all the questions, life experience, and language Hartman and his actors jam into it. It fills to overflowing and explodes.

In this, to cite theatrical precedents, the Gawdafful National Theater is less like the coolly deconstructionist Wooster Group (though it shares their absurdist sensibility and dry wit), and more like the messily sincere Living Theatre. Indeed, when I saw my first GANT play I felt I finally understood, in a visceral way, what it must have been like to experience avant-garde theater in the sixties—to not just be *made aware* by a performance, but to be *changed* by it. As Julian Beck, who cofounded the Living Theatre with Judith Malina in 1947, wrote in his journal in 1959: "I dream of a theatre company, of a company of actors that would stop imitating … that would move the audience in such a way and imbue that audience with such ideas and feeling that transformation and genuine transcendence can be achieved."[2]

Like Antonin Artaud, his inspiration, Beck understood that the conventions of the theater could not—or could no longer—achieve this, especially the conventional language of the theater. Throughout the fifties, the Living Theatre devoted itself to "poetic dramas" or "verse theater," seeking to be as experimental with language as it was with staging and performance. But by the early sixties they had suspended this project: "There has been some theatre verse in the last twenty years that I respect," said Beck, "but not enough, and still too dependent on the verse spirit of other eras to speak directly, engagingly, to the audiences of our time. We wait and work, because when it happens it will happen because we are prepared for it. By 'we' I mean everyone, not only needing it, but wanting it, craving it."[3]

The work Beck and Malina did while waiting for this new language to emerge moved away from scripted texts toward improvisation, ritual, and the preverbal or nonverbal elements of theater. As a director, Malina began "to let the actors design their movements, creating a remarkable rehearsal atmosphere in which the company became more and more free to bring in its own ideas." Through the participatory "body piles" of *Paradise Now* (1968) and other rituals, they worked to free the body from its state of "thinghood"—whether in performing or watching—by producing conditions "in which the public can experience its own physical self, examine its being, its own physical being, its own holy body individually and collectively."[4]

In the late sixties and seventies, the Living Theatre's legendary experiments went even further, into communal living, anarcho-pacifism, and revolutionary politics, as they struggled to create new forms of art that would open out onto new forms of living. But by their own admission, they never quite arrived at the "verse spirit" that could do that same thing. For this, we had to wait for Asher Hartman and his Gawdafful National Theater.

GANT's ambitions are on a par with the Living Theatre's: to resist the contemporary impulse toward "ultra-softness" in the theater, by which Hartman means the avoidance of feeling.[5] This widespread fear of stirring up the audience he views as a "denial of class and privilege," insisting that we push beyond this "surface theater" to the hidden truths we don't want to acknowledge: "the thing that's the thing beneath the thing." This is just as true for his performers: Hartman sees his role in the company as "stretching people to go to places they don't want to go, that I know they're profoundly capable of going, and having them show up there effortlessly."

How is this accomplished? What is the Gawdafful process? To begin with, you should know a few things about Hartman: He is a painter, with a graduate degree from CalArts and an undergraduate degree in theater from UCLA. He has years of teaching experience in both painting and performance. Given his background, his networks and productions are, not surprisingly, transdisciplinary, and his actors hail from the worlds of theater, music, and visual art. Hartman is also an intuitive with a well-established energy reading practice, and his plays and his process actively mine various energistic or affective registers in pursuit of new forms and the redeployment of old ones.

Each play takes six months to a year to develop in rehearsal, with the actors rehearsing three or four times a week, three hours at a time, in Hartman's studio. The plays are written through a back-and-forth between Hartman and company members, with each play "built" on a particular actor or pair of actors. The building

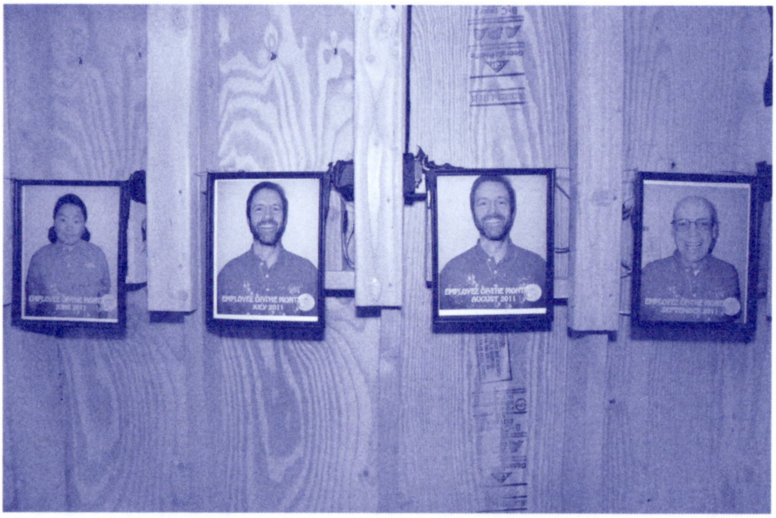

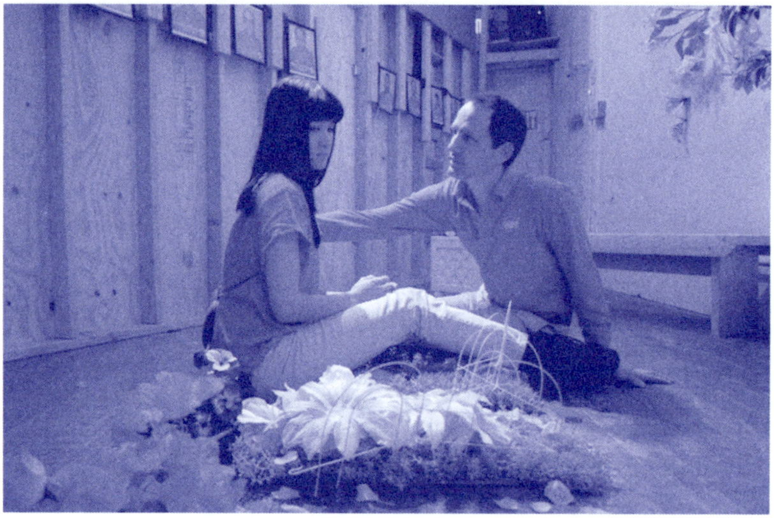

(above) Hallway, set of *See What Love the Father Has Given Us*, Machine Project, Los Angeles, 2012; from left: Haruko Tanaka, Mark Allen, and Michael Morrissey; (below) Rehearsal view, *See What Love the Father Has Given Us*; from left: Ray (Jasmine Orpilla) and Rex (Joe Seely)

process begins with Hartman interviewing them, asking what they want to do, who they want to play, as he derives—or receives—mental images from their answers. He then goes off and "listens" for the characters who emerge, sometimes returning with as many as six hundred pages of "automatic" (for lack of a better word) writing for the company to sift through to find what sits well on the actors. "He takes it all in from us—he's photographing us, in a way, he's doing spiritual photographs," actor Philip Littell explains. "And then he sends the bucket down this deep well. You can hardly hear it strike the water, it's so deep, and up come his texts. They're obscure and dense, but you know the stuff is in there, so you frack it, you apply more process to it—you put it together, take it apart, put it together, take it apart."[6]

These nuggets form the basis of the script, which Hartman continues to revise over the course of the rehearsal process as the company strives to break the habits of contemporary theater via energetic work and exercises, deep meditation, "ancestral mining," and structured improvisations of all sorts. Actor Chelsea Rector describes how empathetic connections are activated among company members, drawing them into one another's energy so as "to get at the unexpected outcome, usually filtered through comedy, violence, or sex." It's a process that "wakes you up, gets you working in your body, gets you in touch with the unseen." As with the Living Theatre, Rector stresses how central the body is to the Gawdafful process overall, noting that everyone in the company has an "articulated movement vocabulary of their own, so we have an understanding of one another at a really physical level." This work *starts* with the body, she insists—"the body in politics, rage, loss, and confusion."

If the work starts with the body and its energies, it ends with poetry. Rector sees Hartman's words as taking on a weight and solidity that's unusual: "I'm talking like I'm moving because the language has such a topography to it." While she concedes that it's demanding on the audience, listening to the work pays off: "You can get a universe of information out of the pieces—and if you ask me, that's the work of poetry." Rector jokes that when she's working

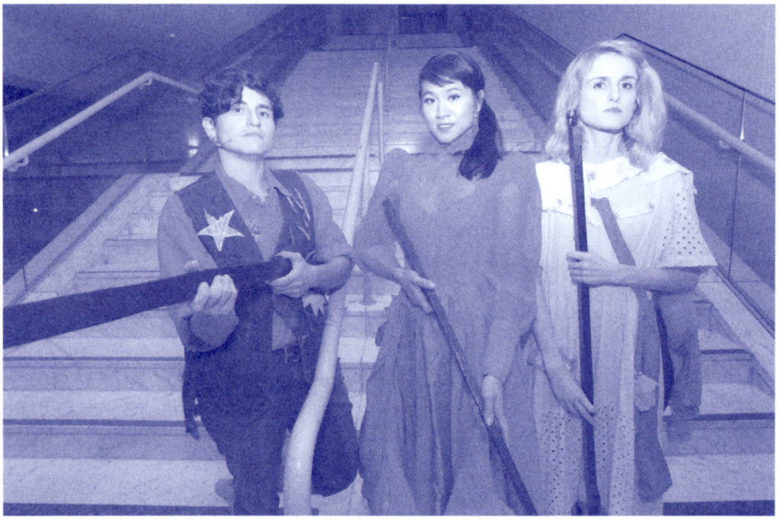

Rehearsal view, *Annie Okay*, Hammer Museum, Los Angeles, 2010; from left: Annie (Dawn Kasper), Annie (Jasmine Orpilla), and Annie (Claire Cronin)

on a Gawdafful play, her family often asks her, "Will the next one be about anything?" Her reaction: "I feel like saying, how do you not understand we're creating your whole world in front of you?" For Littell, Hartman's writing "has the flow of Shakespeare, the density of Stein, and the atmosphere of Beckett." He notes its playfulness on the level of the sentence—"the language is so delicious—[Hartman] will take a phrase or a cliché and scramble it or stick it upside down"—but also emphasizes that it's "deeply felt."

The three plays collected in this volume—*Purple Electric Play (PEP!)*, *Mr. Akita*, and *Sorry, Atlantis: Eden's Achin' Organ Seeks Revenge* (2017)—are the first by Hartman to be published. Can we say what they're about? Perhaps it's better, more fitting, to say what they contain—barely! Somehow, *PEP!* manages to hold Maurice Chevalier, the German Occupation, the French Revolution, vaudeville, TV variety shows of the sixties and early seventies, black-light theater, and *Britain's Got Talent*, to name just a few of its elements, many of which come together in the play's early lines:

*Friends of the Guillotine,*
*Watch as, I, Actor,*
*Step on the stage.*
*The epitome of style,*
*A Man who organizes sleep.*
*You wan' be me, Citizen, no?*
*A Fagin with green lips*
*How to confess the diabolical things I've done.*

*Note the exits front and back, friends,*
*Now is a good time,*
*No harm will come to you …*
*If you're thinking about it …*

If we choose to stay for the performance, we are encouraged, in Hartman's director's notes, to "let the play take [us] through its many layers." As with an energy reading, "meaning is established gradually, cumulatively, and without effort."

*Mr. Akita* is a one-person show featuring a performer, Cliff Hengst, dialoguing with an abstract painting, Emily Joyce's *Sun Burn (Split) 1*. Despite being Hartman's shortest play to date, it nonetheless manages to incorporate Borscht Belt comedy, torch singing, meditations on abstract painting, the figure of the Artist, and the teaching of art, as well as the mysterious dog Mr. Akita, who is at once professor, student, sexual predator, and lover. *Sorry, Atlantis*, Hartman's most recent play, takes on "the spiritual roots of white supremacy, misogyny, and fascism as it plays out in contemporary American society." As Hartman's notes go on to explain, it "combine[s] the aesthetics of pre-war and WWII cartooning, archetypes of Greek mythology, the psychosexual underbelly of Jungian psychoanalysis, and gay and Shakespearean camp."

In these plays, the visual writing is as layered and arresting and slyly irreverent as the text. *Sorry, Atlantis*'s floor-to-ceiling ramped stage, for instance, with well-positioned holes in the floor from which the various performers pop up, creates a suffocating feeling of no exit; the actors risk bumping their heads against a brutal ceiling when they try to stand and walk around. The dancing consumer product-puppets of *PEP!* (disposable diapers, a pizza box, Kleenex, a Big Gulp) come to life in a magical display of commodity capitalism; at play's end, Mother Theater's giant pneumatic purple tongue lunges from the stage to lick the audience. In *Mr. Akita*, the op-art sun of Joyce's painting is a recurring image, all the way through to the play's closing lines:

> *The Painting's wound spreads, sun-like.*
>
> *Teacher says:*
> *What is a sun?*
> *Can anyone tell me?*
> *Can anyone tell me?*
> *Yes? Akita?*
>
> "A sun is the object that rages back."
> *"Well, that's not quite right," teacher says.*
> *"But you're very close."*

The long-awaited publication of Hartman's plays in this volume raises the question of iterability. Are these plays, built on specific actors using a specific process, able to be performed by anybody else? The Gawdafful National Theater contains multitudes: Its casts are always multiracial, multigenerational, multigendered, and multisexual—and of course, open to having their psyches mined. In performance, they are, as Rector says, "strong and flexible enough to pull the affect out of the language."

Then there's the issue of setting to consider: For several years, GANT was in residency at the legendary Los Angeles alternative space Machine Project, where founder Mark Allen encouraged Hartman to transform the building to fit the needs of each production, making them in some sense site-specific. The Machine Project space closed in 2018, but Littell isn't worried about having the work taken up in other contexts, by other actors. "The excitement of 'having book,'" he says, "is that people will get the wrong idea, but imaginatively—the way we all got the wrong idea about Jerzy Grotowski from those grainy photographs. They excited us."

There's much to be excited about in this book, which opens up new horizons for the theater and its language, and also for ways of coming together as we face an increasingly turbulent future. Philosopher and psychoanalyst Cornelius Castoriadis understood art's mission to be "the exploration of ever new strata of the psyche and the social, of the visible and the audible" in order to give form to chaos,[7] which feels like a good description of the work of the Gawdafful National Theater. In our chaotic times, too often rendered in dangerously simplistic terms, the company's vital and complex excavations, captured here in the "verse spirit" of Asher Hartman, are a radical and necessary intervention.

Janet Sarbanes is the author of two short fiction collections, *Army of One* (2008) and *The Protester Has Been Released* (2017), and numerous writings on art and politics, including the forthcoming essay collection *Letters on the Autonomy Project*.

1
Asher Hartman's Gawdafful National Theater website, https://gawdafful nationaltheater.company, accessed on September 14, 2018.

2
John Tytell, *The Living Theatre: Art, Exile, and Outrage* (New York: Grove Press, 1995), 161.

3
Ibid.

4
Julian Beck, "Body," in *The Life of the Theater* (San Francisco: Limelight Editions, 1986), 59.

5
Asher Hartman's comments in this essay are drawn from my conversations with him in May 2018 and from the director's notes he provided me with at that time.

6
The comments of Gawdafful National Theater members Philip Littell and Chelsea Rector in this essay are drawn from my conversations with them in June 2018.

7
Cornelius Castoriadis, "Culture in a Democratic Society," in *The Castoriadis Reader*, ed. and trans. David Ames Curtis (Oxford: Blackwell Publishing, 1997), 345.

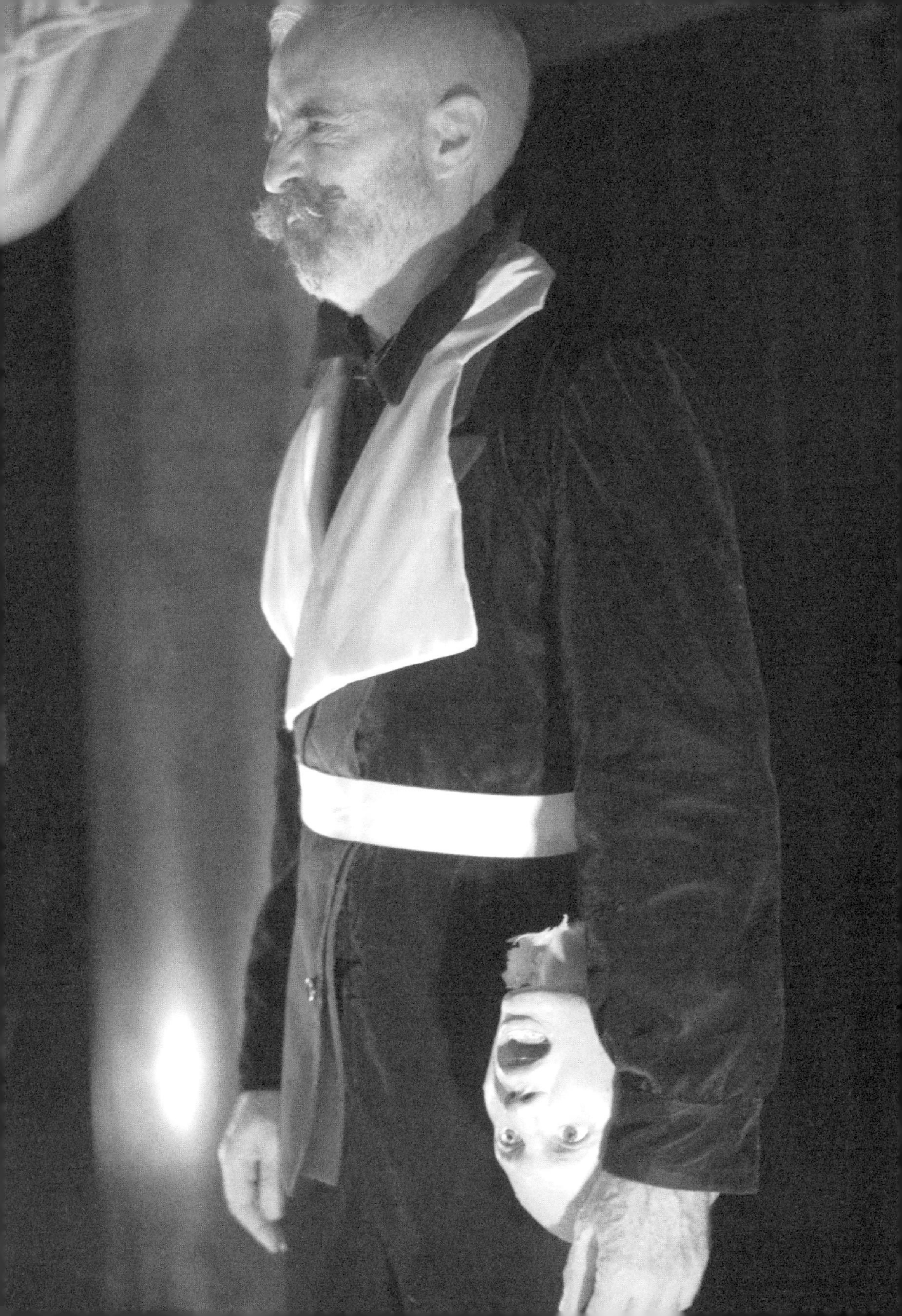

# Dramaturgy for Thespians

Lucas Wrench

Once you've seen Performance Art Face, it can't be unseen. It's the blank expression worn by artists in front of an audience, the facial equivalent to white gallery walls, Marina Abramović's famous *The Artist Is Present* face. Performance Art Face connotes seriousness, but also neutrality, and maybe a kind of communism. PAF, often accompanied by uniform-style monochromatic garb, attempts to obscure the performer as a stand-in, or body double, or some other kind of universal stripped of personality and class background. It's not about the individual. They are simply there to execute the action—whether that's sitting motionless at a table, or submitting to ritualistic bloodletting.

Asher Hartman does not utilize PAF. The performers of the Gawdafful National Theater are not untrained bodies, engaged in some gesture, but highly skilled actors, pulling from their experience to deliver dense and complex lines of dialogue with precisely calibrated inflection and expression. Hartman's performers spend months cultivating absurd Victorian moustache stylings; they're costumed in thick velvet and finely tailored suits. The characters they embody are written precisely for each actor, with Hartman drawing from a decade-plus of psychic practice to craft characters that engage with who these actors are as people, how they see themselves, and how the world sees them. Hartman's performances don't happen in interchangeable white-walled galleries. They demand months of modifications and construction—the trapdoors go *here*, the audience sits *there*.

These are tactics familiar to theater, but Hartman's work is presented in art spaces, to primarily art audiences. If there is recognizable imagery, or distinct narrative, it seems specifically crafted for those in attendance—tales of grizzled art instructors,

Marat's bloated arm, creative-class dilettantes with revolutionary ambitions ... Accordingly, the patrons of the Gawdafful National Theater come from contemporary art worlds, and lack influence over the theatrical institutions accustomed to presenting works of this scale and complexity. The result is a continuous uphill struggle. The company's members labor to develop infrastructure that comes standard in theatrical venues (spotlights, curtains, a bar, a box office ... ), in order to present experimental plays to audiences who require repeated reassurance that they will not be touched or summoned to the stage.

The friction Hartman encounters is part of a long-standing tension between performance art and theater, most dogmatically expressed by Yvonne Rainer in 1965: "NO to spectacle no to virtuosity no to transformations and magic and make-believe."[1] The "NO Manifesto" reads as a point-by-point denial of everything I love in Hartman's work, but Rainer speaks to a legitimate skepticism toward these kinds of tactics—a recognition of the very real exploitation that runs machines of fantasy and spectacle. "No to the glamour and transcendency of the star image." Or to quote the Vital Organ II, from the Gawdafful production *Purple Electric Play (PEP!)* (2014), "I'll miss the hard self-hatred across every young girl's brow, and all the nasty, dirty sex, plastic film, and the feeling that whatever happens, there'll be a comeback."

Rainer was observing a deeply hierarchical dance world dominated by rigid apprenticeships, burn-out track careers, and lavish productions bankrolled by the very wealthiest of patrons. "NO Manifesto" offered a vision for a more visceral and essential performance—radically scaled back and disinterested in displays of technical ability—that could be created without significant resources or years of sacrifice for the development of a narrow skill set. Broadly speaking, it is a model that has come to distinguish performance art from more mainstream forms of live entertainment. Its venues prioritize clean neutrality over performance infrastructure and amenities. Artists will occasionally hire actors, dancers, or other trained performers, but it's rare to find a performance artist engaged in the type of virtuosity that more material-based

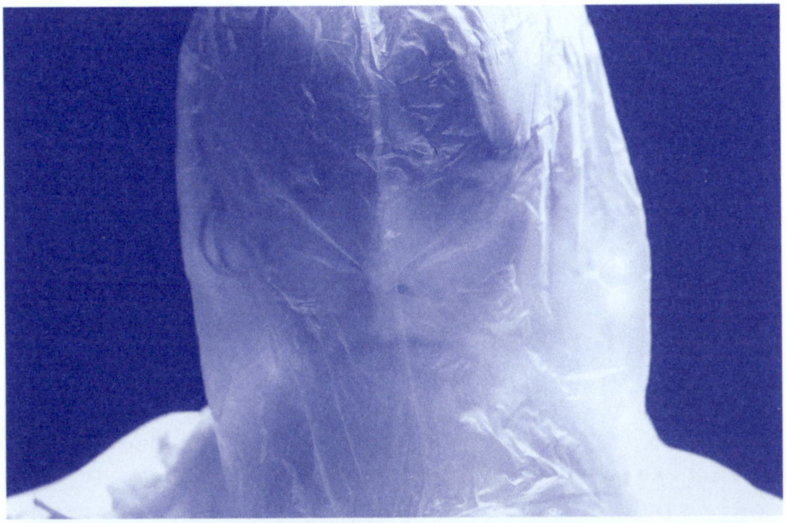

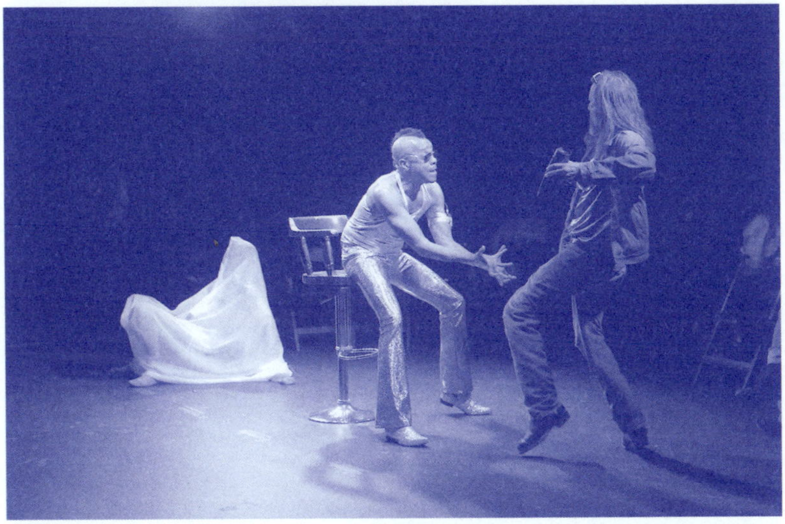

Rehearsal views, *The Silver, the Black, the Wicked Dance*, Los Angeles County Museum of Art (LACMA), 2016; (above) Raccoon (Chelsea Rector); (below) from left: White Alien (Philip Littell), Forced Entertainer (Paul Outlaw), and Trapper (Joe Seely)

art practices like painting and sculpture are built on. The removal of the entire floor of the Machine Project space for Gawdafful's *Sorry, Atlantis: Eden's Achin' Organ Seeks Revenge* (2017) was the type of flashy expense that runs counter to performance art's egalitarianism. *PEP!*'s soundboard manipulated us with its ringing high notes and trembling bass. It's valid to resist such tricks of the stage, and Hartman met with no shortage of pushback for his efforts.

Rainer's restraint, or the respectful impassivity of Performance Art Face, echoes an asceticism described by Ursula K. Le Guin in her short story "Solitude" (1994), where a deeply isolated community has determined that "to live rightly a person has to keep away from magic."[2] But Le Guin goes further, homing in on the slippage between the mechanism of manipulation and the manipulation itself. As the protagonist tries to explain, *technology isn't magic*; magic is using "power to get power over other persons."

In 2018, when Hartman came to the Philbrook Museum of Art in Tulsa, Oklahoma, for a version of Krystal Krunch's (Asher Hartman and Haruko Tanaka's) Intro to Mind Reading workshop, it was this charge of manipulation that sparked controversy. Atheists and Christians alike admonished the museum for defrauding its audience with supernatural claims. Danwade1 commented on Instagram: "It's the same as if the Philbrook hosted faith healers or flat earthers. I do feel it cheapens [the museum's] reputation a bit." For those who know Hartman, or don't know Oklahoma, this reaction seems absurd, but it's notable that two of his primary disciplines—live theater and psychic practice—are defined in the eyes of many as disingenuous and exploitative.

*Two paintings walked into a bar.*
*The first said, Gimme a thrill.*
*The other said, Gimme all your money, your life, your mind, your would-be children, your hope against hope; your self-esteem; your crouching, servile sense of time; the ability to orient yourself in space, the knowledge that you've soiled your adult diapers, you don't have much time left, and you didn't make the grade.*[3]

The dynamic of the stage as a site of exploitation is implicit to vaudeville, a historic genre Hartman appropriates liberally. In vaudeville, arguably the last truly mainstream live-performance form, performers strain themselves both physically and emotionally in pursuit of entertainment. In its heyday in early-twentieth-century America, vaudeville involved legitimate threats to life and limb—theater fires sparked by hot sodium lights, an errant throwing knife … European immigrants churned their daily traumas and mundane poverty into crude stereotypes to the delight of large audiences. Cinema added new pressures: Performances captured on film could tour on their own, eliminating costly live acts. The most infamous of these degradations, and likely vaudeville's most lasting contribution, was the popularization of blackface. In this culture of desperation, both white and black performers were working in blackface by vaudeville's final days. The enduring popularity of these racist caricatures provided one of the few remaining avenues to making a living onstage.

Hartman's plays are populated with vaudevillians—tragic, archaic talents, on a tour that might be their last. Cliff Hengst plays a Borscht-Belt-comedian-turned-talking-dog in *Mr. Akita* (2015). Philip Littell is deployed as *PEP!*'s somewhat slimy curtain puller ("Here, my darling actors, is the Thing we've been waiting for, ready to be abused by your mania for attention"). Desperate eagerness to entertain permeates the Gawdafful productions, populated with prop-gags, dance breaks, and musical interludes meant to occupy a restless audience between acts. In one short scene in *PEP!*, the Star pulls a piece of wood from offstage—"They're *bored*!" he exclaims. A white afro wig and a Zen monk puppet come next—"They are *fro*-zen!" It's a moment of pure silliness direct from vaudeville. Likewise, the giant glittering tongue that emerges at the play's finale borrows the "effect finish," when an elaborate and as-yet-unseen prop ends the show.

But before the tongue comes out, there's one last song: "When you die every day / And no one sees your pain … " So croons a popcorn-bucket puppet named Donkey. Its mouth is ragged, barely held together by fleshy bandages—a record of the nightly beating about to ensue.

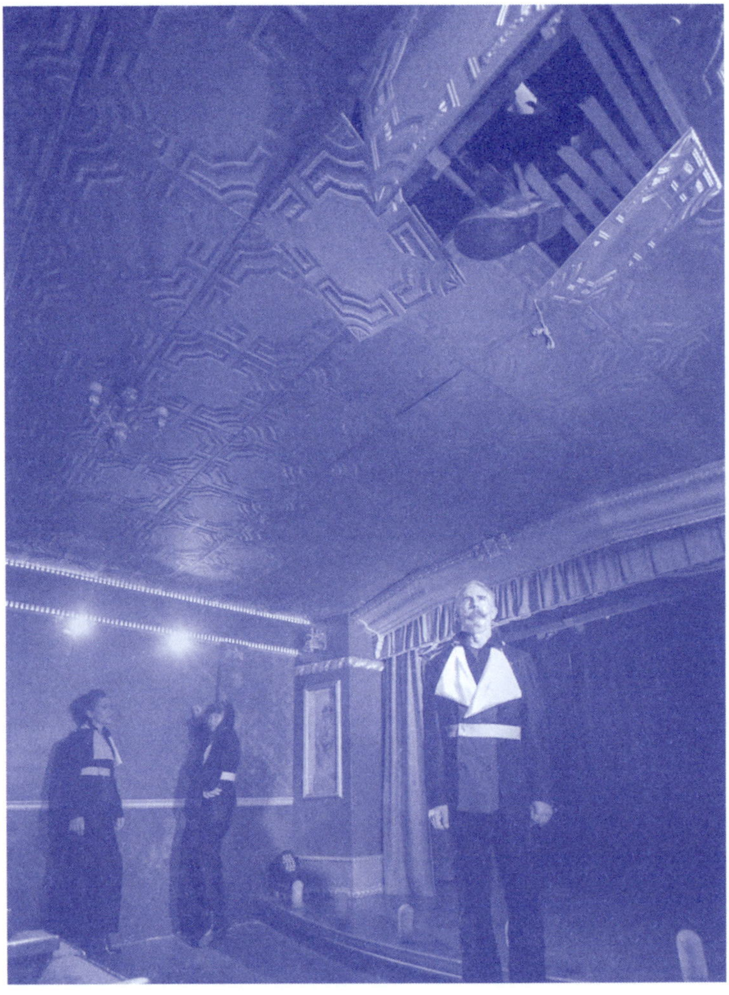

Rehearsal view, *Purple Electric Play (PEP!)*, Machine Project, Los Angeles, 2014; counter-clockwise from lower left: Vital Organ II (Kalean Ung), Vital Organ (Jasmine Orpilla), Star (Philip Littell), and Boot

Hartman has immersed himself in an ethically fraught set of disciplines, and his characters' fates reflect this. This work requires the long-term maintenance of trust across vulnerable relationships; the marshalling of significant resources; not to mention the logistical and organizational challenge of producing multi-month runs. All while avoiding the kinds of magic that should be avoided.

What Hartman offers is, to borrow from Krystal Krunch, a kind of re-enchantment, repurposing this set of tools—theater with its nightly deaths, its love of rehearsal and repetition; vaudevillian charm; psychic mediation—into a means for exploring cycles of trauma and healing. *What is life but violation and recovery?*[4] This work assures, much more.

> *Qui est le peuple, you ask? The people carve out an existence. My body has been used as a site of pleasure, as a bag of wheat, as a source of feeling, as raw energy, but rarely have you glimpsed the depths of the love I am capable of lifting out of life. Qui est le peuple? I don't know. But I possess here the item that unites us: from the Mother: La Dent! The Tooth! The Bone! And I will use it to light up the world!*[5]

(Lights flicker. Black out.)

Lucas Wrench was Machine Project's operations manager (2014-17) and associate curator (2015-17). He now lives in Oklahoma as a Tulsa Artist Fellow.

1
"NO Manifesto," first published in Yvonne Rainer, "Some Retrospective Notes on a Dance for 10 People and 12 Mattresses Called Parts of Some Sextets, Performed at the Wadsworth Atheneum, Hartford, Connecticut, and Judson Memorial Church, New York, in March, 1965," *Tulane Drama Review* 10, no. 2 (Winter 1965); repr. in Yvonne Rainer, *Works 1961-73* (Halifax: Nova Scotia College of Art and Design, 1974), 51.

2
Ursula K. Le Guin, "Solitude," *The Magazine of Fantasy and Science Fiction*, December 1994.

3
Asher Hartman, *Mr. Akita*.

4
Ibid.

5
Asher Hartman, *Purple Electric Play (PEP!)*.

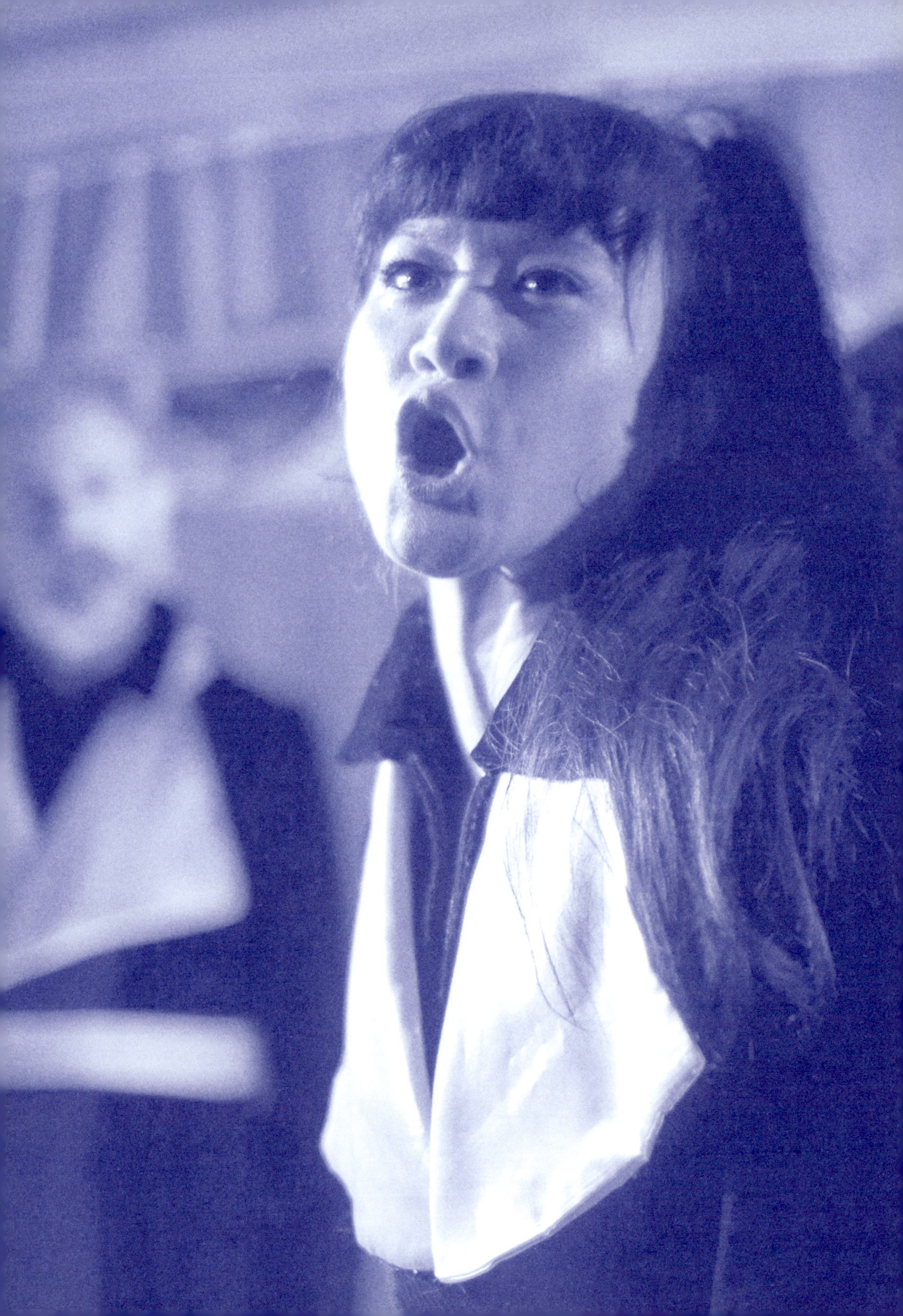

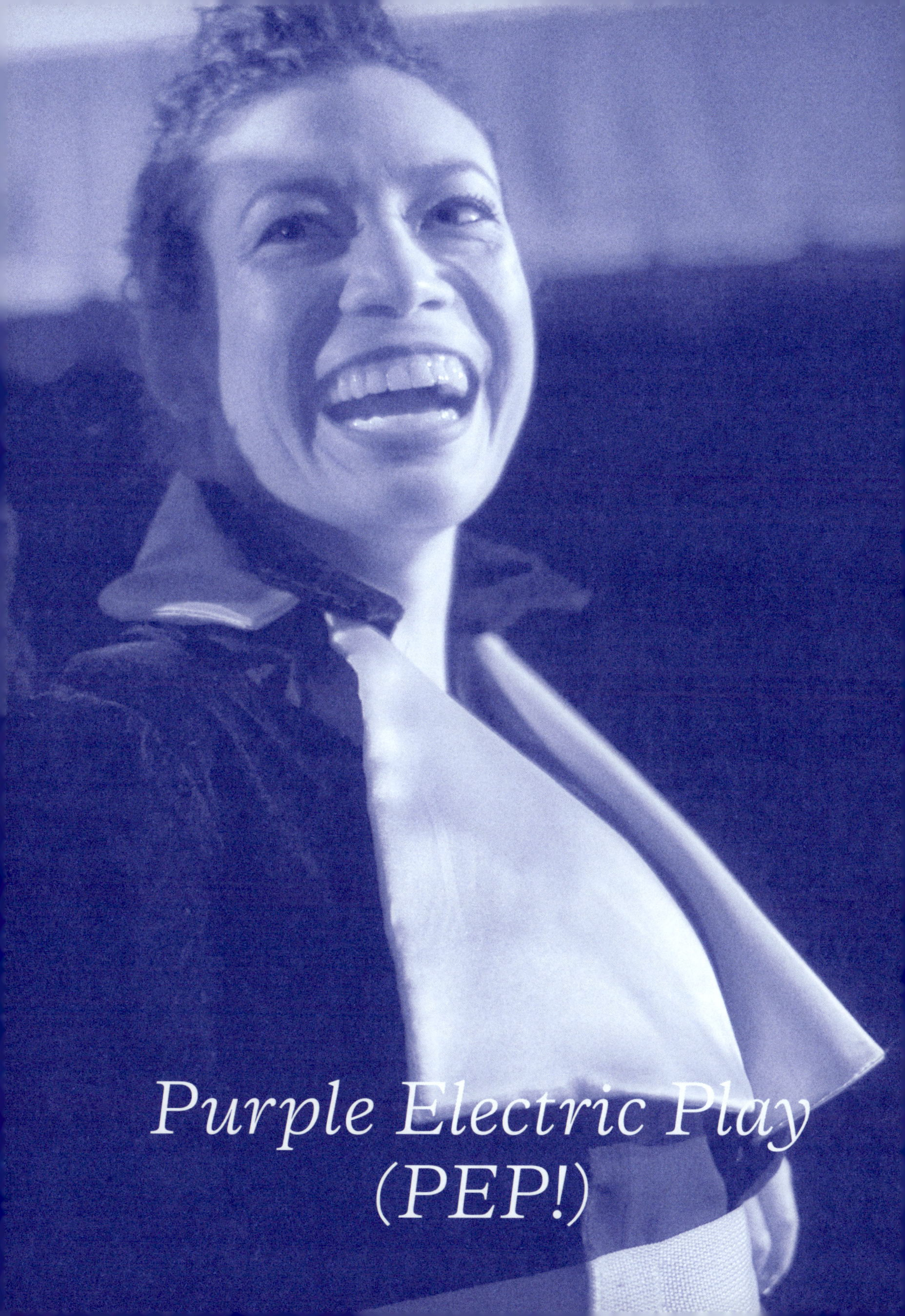

# *Purple Electric Play (PEP!)*

Written and directed by Asher Hartman

First performed at Machine Project, Los Angeles, October 30, 2014
Assistant Director: Zut Alors

VITAL ORGAN . . . . . . . . . . . . . . . . . . . . . . . . . . . . . . . . . . Jasmine Orpilla
VITAL ORGAN II . . . . . . . . . . . . . . . . . . . . . . . . . . . . . . . . . . Kalean Ung
STAR, a comedian . . . . . . . . . . . . . . . . . . . . . . . . . . . . . . Philip Littell
AUDIENCE, a bird . . . . . . . . . . . . . . . . . . . . . . . . . . . . . . . . Joe Seely
SONGBIRD . . . . . . . . . . . . . . . . . . . . . . . . . . . . . . . . . Drew Thataussie
MAD SHADOW . . . . . . . . . . . . . . . . . . . . . . . . . . . . . . . . Chelsea Rector
CHANCE HAPPENSTANCE . . . . . . . . . . . . . . . . . . . . . . . . . . . idle actor

PUPPETS: MONKEY doll, very small, half asleep; DIRECTOR doll; SALAD BAR, large kale or lettuce leaf; LO-PHAT, cup of yogurt; DONKEY, box of popcorn in wheelchair; STARVATION, cup of ramen; BOARD; WHITE AFRO; ZEN MONK; X and BIRD; BLOODY DECAPITATED HEAD; EARS; EYES; TOOTH; white PAPER HORSE; SQUIRREL; BOOT attached to human leg; LARGE FLOPPY ARM WITH YELLOW QUILL PEN, like Jacques-Louis David's *Death of Marat*; PAMPERS BOX; old BIG GULP CUP; PIZZA BOX; KLEENEX BOX; MOTHER THEATER'S TONGUE

*The audience enters a barren storefront. A young man sits at a table, taking names. When not interacting, he plays a game of hangman.*

*They are led down an old staircase and into a cramped basement with plush seating, a false ceiling, and a small curtained stage (concealing a miniature black velvet theater, for puppetry and magic). This basement theater brings to mind the Victorian era, yet with a hint of Constructivist bite in its decor, or, if you like, a nod to Marie Antoinette's private theater at Versailles, albeit of slightly thinner budget. The audience takes their seats, joined by Vital Organ II.*

*Star enters—stoic, elegant. He steps into the audience and moves about mwah-kissing. ("I'm sorry, so sorry, my dear. Condolences. Be brave. Love you. Pardon. Excuse me. I'm so sorry.") Exits. The curtains are yanked open to reveal Vital Organ with electric guitar. House lights up. She plays—an open chord, a riff. Curtains drop.*

*Star appears in the drawn curtains as spotlit face.*

**STAR**
Mesdames, Messieurs,
I am a little mouse.
Terrified, silent, remote.

*Warm light all over. Vital Organ crosses stage in a gallop.*

**VITAL ORGAN**
*(In French)*
I am sure I am the total package.
The perfect robot to combat degradation and shame.
Alas, I win! Every time!

*Star steps forward, covering chest with curtain like a Roman patrician.*

**STAR**
*(French, proclaiming)*
I am sure I am the perfect product,
The perfect arrangement of the senses to combat the forces against me.

*(Bad French accent)*
I travel.

*Vital Organ enters again as horse, sees she has the wrong timing, turns around.*

But I am not here.
Do not watch me.
If you watch, you will come to love me,
And in the end be hurt, terribly.
Because I will fail.
What will be done to me is so inconceivable, so shocking (that)
Your eyes, your lovely eyes, cannot bear that vision to craft.
Thus, I beg you, love, do not love, do not see.
Don't look.

*Star exits. Curtains go up. Vital Organ crosses into audience, returns to stage.*

**VITAL ORGAN**
*(Smart alecky)*
Collaborators,
The theater is
A shit factory for beginners
A dumb trick's asshole.
Watch the blade, silly rabbit,
The invisible blade, because it is always
Suspended ...

*She looks up, tokes.*

... on high.

*Soft creaking sound. Star enters robotically.*

**STAR**
*(Electronic)*
And now,
Nobles, for your pleasure I prevent myself from feeling.

*Star bounces on one leg. Vital Organ joins him. They begin to dance Eddie Cantor–like.*

I keep myself hygienically close but at the same time distant ...
Not to bother, only charm.

O, lady!
Merde, where all dese people comin' from!

*Music (bluesy Caribbean, Chevalier). From wings, cymbal-playing hands appear. Vital Organ plays bongo, deadpan.*

*(Singing)*
Down, down in old country
M'arm came wid a block of bees
Bees, bees, dese blackest bees
How they drunk and prick and pee!
Oh green, green de sea
Now dey wan' my sympat'y
What brazen ass, what mare donkey!
Push dem out her damn pussy
Oh black, dese blackest bees
Day done eat down my dynasty
Now dey want dem wide-screen TV
Oh, merde! Absurdity
Come on, man, RSVP
Get them out them out my damn country
A funeral for dem all!

*Star makes three gestures of self-destruction, claps enthusiastically.*

Citoyens! Citoyens! Citoyens!
Let us be terrible so the people won't have to be!

**VITAL ORGAN**
*(Flat)*
Jesters are by nature cruel.

Jesters want mankind to fail.

*All peek out from wings.*

Jesters are a moral threat to the innocent who, otherwise unexposed to jesters, would have more productive evenings.

**STAR**

*(Jaunty, diabolical)*

Lovers, Amours,
Friends of the Guillotine,
Watch as, I, Actor,
Step on the stage.
The epitome of style,
A man who organizes sleep.
You wan' be me, Citizen, no?
A Fagin with green lips.
How to confess the diabolical things I've done.

*Star moves arms like a flight attendant.*

Note the exits front and back, friends,
Now is a good time,
No harm will come to you ...
If you're thinking about it ...

*Vital Organ becomes Bunraku puppet speaking singsong. Songbird enters and, with Star, lifts Vital Organ from underneath her arms. Star sets her ankle, Songbird poses her.*

**VITAL ORGAN**

*(Stiffly)*

I ... am ...
Led out onto the stage,
Foot buckling,
Before an audience of estimable men.
I, the Vital Organ, populated by slosh and revenge.
Step forward.
The audience bites their collective lip.
"Tragically we have enough to see but not enough to eat," say they, their mouths crammed full.

*Light becomes dreamy, narcotic—blues, purples, reds.*

**STAR**

*(A showman, Dracula)*

And now! Everything you see and experience here will be real!

*Audience and Songbird lift Vital Organ again—she appears to float.*

Like a movie or a floating picture,
You will observe as if from behind glass.
Nothing will affect you that hasn't already.
You will go down—

**VITAL ORGAN**

Down, down ... down.

*They drop Vital Organ.*

**STAR**
*(Breathing heavily)*
Imagine that we are huddled together.
Pack animals, respiring after the hunt.

*Vital Organ and Star walk into audience as if they are pack animals.*

**VITAL ORGAN**
*(Panting)*
They above. We below, together.

*Monkey appears in black velvet theater—pen in hand.*

*(Pointing)*
See!

*Director appears.*

The director, lolling, with pen in hand, in the back row,
Measuring every word, ready to yank the show if he has to!

*Monkey is off on "has to."*

**STAR**
Citizen Theater, boards, curtains, lights, prepare!

**VITAL ORGAN**
*(Hint of jaundice)*
They kill for pleasure you know.

**STAR**
*(Naively)*
Sure. I know.

**VITAL ORGAN**
You wanna drink?

**STAR**
What'ya got?

*Purple lights flash. Star and Vital Organ glance above while pliéing in alternation—two Chaplin-esque characters. Music ("La Dee Da").*

**VITAL ORGAN**
Purple.

*(Bad French accent)*
Ça va, Monsieur L'Etoile?

**STAR**
*(Bad French accent)*
Ça va, Monsieur Le Coeur.
Is the weather foul or fair?

**VITAL ORGAN**
The weather is obscured by the sky, Monsieur.

**STAR**
How do you find it?

**VITAL ORGAN**
By looking up.

**STAR**
*(Mildly amused)*
Ah, ha. Here's hoping it rains, for rain clarifies.

**VITAL ORGAN II**
*(From audience, sotto voce)*
It's blood that clarifies, Monsieur.

**VITAL ORGAN**
It's blood that clarifies, Monsieur.

**STAR**
To be replaced by light I am sure.

*Star levitates.*

The natural
O-o-o-rder!

**VITAL ORGAN**
As natural as gravity.

*Star falls to ground. Gets up.*

**STAR**
Regard, her temper is not to be believed.
Watch this!

*Snare sound. Vital Organ "re-enters," slinks toward Star, poses with jutted hip, bats eyes.*

Ah ... where are you going?

**VITAL ORGAN**
*(Soft, flirty)*
Nowhere.

*Bump-bump! Drumbeat over snare to the rhythm of Vital Organ's hips ("The Bump," '70s).*

**STAR**
*(Turned on, Johnny Carson-like)*
Mmm ... I wonder.

**VITAL ORGAN**
Gonna get me some ...

*Bump-bump!*

Peace.

**STAR**
*(Tightens imaginary tie, clears throat)*

You want it all to stop, do you now?

*Bump-bump! Star juts hips.*

**VITAL ORGAN**
Uh-huh.

**STAR**
It seems to me ... it's gotta go on.

**VITAL ORGAN**
*(Bats eyes, pouts)*
Oh.

**STAR**
Sure.
Why, here are our friends now!

*Enter Salad Bar, Lo-Phat, Donkey, and Starvation. Puppet sounds and applause.*

Have you all come to see the show?

**PUPPETS**
Yes, sir. Yes. Why, yes! Yeah!

**VITAL ORGAN**
To visit us?!

**PUPPETS**
Uh-huh!

**STAR**
Well, now that's fine. Tell us, Lo-Phat, do you think we ought to be silent?

**LO-PHAT**
*(Boombox spitting)*
Pff-ts-ts, Pff-ts-ts, Pff, Pff, Pff ...

**STAR**
I see. And you, Salad Bar? Do you agree with me that we oughta find some common ground?

**SALAD BAR**
*(Strained, high-pitched, snickering)*
Che Cosa fai?

**STAR**
Not you too, Donkey?

*Donkey shakes, loses popcorn. Cymbals sound. Canned laughter.*

Now there's a shakedown I can get behind.

**VITAL ORGAN**
Starvation, you know what I want?

**STAR**
*(Rockin', bass)*
You know what I want?
I want peace

*Exit Lo-Phat.*

You know what I want?
I want peace

*Music (Euro-style disco). Purple light—narcotic, revolving patterns.*

I want a piece peace piece
Piece of the action
Gimme gimme gimme gimme gimme some reaction!

*Starvation and Salad Bar groove. Star and Vital Organ dance and lip-synch.*

**VITAL ORGAN**
*(Rockin', sexy)*
You know what I want
I want love
You know what I want
I want love
I got love love love love love love
Love of the action
Gimme gimme gimme gimme gimme some some of that action.

*Audience's head appears between curtains—menacing, strange. Disappears. Star shudders, tentatively parts curtains. No one is there. Audience appears again, curtain rope over shoulder and golf club and ball in hand. He gives them to Star, who is unsure, wary.*

**VITAL ORGAN**
And so you went about your way.

**STAR**
*(Practicing putting)*
Yes.

*Vital Organ cautiously approaches.*

**VITAL ORGAN**
You stole glances at yourself in store windows.

**STAR**
Occasionally. True.

**VITAL ORGAN**
You posted a few items—

**VITAL ORGAN II**
*(From audience)*
Nothing too political.

**STAR**
Hmm.

**VITAL ORGAN**
Your muscles grew increasingly lax.

**STAR**
*(Hurt, looking at gut)*
Oh!

**VITAL ORGAN**
You gave orders. Got a little personal with the stick.

**STAR**
Well.

**VITAL ORGAN II**
Tricky with the lingo to mystify the folks in the back—

**STAR**
For the love of the art, you know—

**VITAL ORGAN**
No one could quite understand you.

**STAR**
*(Head down)*
(It's) Not for everyone.

**VITAL ORGAN**
Except that your outrage grew—

**STAR**
Inwardly, true.

**VITAL ORGAN**
And people began to disappear.

STAR
*(Mocking, dark)*
People?

*Music ("O Lazarus"). Star moves into audience.*

VITAL ORGAN
*(In French—singing, high, pure)*
Lazarus, O Lazarus,
Now is the time to get up!
O Lazarus, out of that crypt!!
They've left without you, fool
The revolution has begun.

STAR
*(Confrontational, needling)*
All right, what's your name, darling?

VITAL ORGAN
My name is Susan Boyle.

STAR
Okay, Susan, where you are from?

VITAL ORGAN
I'm from a place from ... from ... you know, babbity-boo, Scottish name, Shangra-la. Tra la. Babbity-boo.

STAR
It's a big town?

VITAL ORGAN
It's a collection of ... it's a collection of ... uh ... ba, ba, ba ...

AUDIENCE
*(From offstage)*
Villages.

VITAL ORGAN
... villages. I had to think there.

STAR
And how old are you, Susan?

VITAL ORGAN
I am 47.

*Sound of laughter.*

And that's just one side of me!

**STAR**
Okay, what's the dream?

**VITAL ORGAN**
I'm trying to be a professional singer.

**STAR**
And why hasn't it worked out so far, Susan?

**VITAL ORGAN**
I don't know, I guess, a host of ... a conflation of ... a systemic arrangement of ... brought by ... a history ... of a history ... of ...

**STAR**
Right. Hit it.

**VITAL ORGAN**
Skinny bitches, I'm afraid of you. You don't have the hip to host the weight of the world, bitches. You don't have the mouth to take it in, BUT I DO. I hate the dry bitch who wants everything just so. Because it is not so! I'm tired of feel-good people. Why don't you know that love hurts? It takes everything right out of you. Everything! You can't give love without having been left. And I've been left bitches ... yeah, I've been left.

**STAR**
Stump. Creature. Abhorrence. What are you some kind of solution, some kind of denouement?

**VITAL ORGAN**
No man, I'm the beginning, I'm the pulp, the whip, the blowback.

*Star jumps onstage—like Al Jolson, up-with-the-people-style.*

**STAR**
*(Jazzy)*
I wish I were hungry like you. So hungry that nothing would fail me!

**VITAL ORGAN**
*(Pissed off)*
Hunger. Hungry. Hunger.

*Vital Organ gives Star the fist and exits. Harp sounds.*

**STAR**
*(As Sir John Gielgud, highbrow, to audience)*

*Enter Large Floppy Arm With Yellow Quill Pen. It floats and rocks.*

Have you ever dreamt of Corday?
Her moderate resolve?
That steady hand?
Wouldn't you too like to make the slit
In the heart of the Giant,
The Paranoiac,
The Crowd?
Goliath of Indifference,
Monster of Dull Intonations,
Clammy predictable Death,
That *the Beast* in a monosyllable proffers?

*(Becomes himself, straightforward)*
I pretend to love the world out of a great shame
  that I do not.
In particular I find the people rotten.
I need not enumerate their vices.
Am I right, actors, that this world is a piss pot
  of one against the other?

*Clown horn. Audience enters driving buggy carrying Vital Organ sitting over Songbird's white-stockinged legs.*

*(Kneeling, saint-like)*
But wait! Your road to Damascus appears.

*(Lewdly, comic like Groucho)*
I may become a follower.

*Vital Organ II comes alive.*

**VITAL ORGAN II**
Comedians, you came down from the slopes
  with your perfect craniums
Bowling balls with three deep holes,
Wells of information to stretch my talons into—

*Vital Organ becomes filled with Vital Organ II's electric energy. Her arms and fingers dance as if releasing acid raindrops. Star eats Vital Organ's/Songbird's white toes.*

**STAR**
*(Chewing)*
Corpus mysticum
Your beautiful legs, the gateway to God
Mon Dieu!
Your open legs, the battlefield,
Spread out across continents
How I desire to be at your heel
Servant of the She-Devil, le Roi
Male-mocked soul
Container of what we don't know
And never want to
Let me eat of you!

**VITAL ORGAN II**
My fingers play the lewd clown's brain
Leaving traces of vengeance there.

**STAR**
Look how suddenly pure you are
How tasty and divine
As the columns of Greece ...
Now I shall replace
Her toes with my teeth
Her body is worth nothing
All fat and sugar
Spun air.

*Star eats. Audience smacks lips. Star is suddenly poisoned. He chokes and is dragged off.*

*Sound of raindrop. Lights go dark—eerie.*

**VITAL ORGAN**
*(A la Lamballe, princess in court of Louis XVI)*
It was in a heavenly downpour that I first realized my comeuppance. Heretofore I'd been shielded, sticking my foot from beneath my parasol when I wanted to laugh with the cold. And then ...

*Star and Audience enter with large, raised, stained cloth spread across stage's width.*

It was quite by accident that my foot caught rain. It had been unshielded for an instant, when ... it stayed and nothing I could do would pull it back.

*They move slightly closer.*

As much as I tried, nothing would retract it. It was at that moment that I realized, *I had enjoyed it*. I had played with the luxury of my heel, my jitters, my love of fine things, and dared to laugh at the rain—the rain, previously an infinite host, became a sea of angry men ...

*They inch forward, menacingly.*

... who stabbed at me, pulled off my clothes, drug me through the streets, and made sure of my sick, my humiliation.

*Star and Audience wrap Vital Organ in cloth as she speaks, eventually placing her wrapped body over their knees.*

I trusted that my own good nature would help me out, me, this dandelion in the dark, this spreader of cheer—the Thing that pursued I could never understand ...

**STAR, VITAL ORGAN, AUDIENCE**
*(Singing)*
If you're not poor

Help is an indignity
If you're not poor
Love is a sometime sentiment
If you're not poor
You can withhold violence
You can look away
Choosing when to give charity or scorn
Choosing not to abuse or take advantage
But when you're poor
You must keep going
You must thrust and hide

**VITAL ORGAN**

But I believe in the end, I shall escape. When I walk to my sedan at night, I shall be the special case, the one upon whom the light does not fall, the one of no consequence, protected by the special fact my shadow is not seen.

*Natural light. Star and Audience toss off Vital Organ.*

**STAR**

Well, I've seen enough, quite enough.

*(Sulking, to audience)*

Fops! You pretend not to know me.

*(Connecticut character, frightened)*

Okay, let's try this again. Why, just the other day ... just the other day, at the wine bar, you remember, the conversation we had, each nodding seriously, about the fact that it *is* coming, as if we were its parents, cautiously, sternly, bringing it about, each concealing our terror, and panic. Actors!

*Star gestures as if to say, "What?" Recoils, hisses, spits.*

**VITAL ORGAN II**

*(Not impressed)*

Actors. Actors. Actors.

*(To audience)*

It's very hard to love, isn't it? I'm talking not 'bout liking someone, or of having a feeling, but of being in a state of mind where all you can do is embrace, because the Being, the poor slob, is terminal. The impulse ...

*Star pouts, raspberries.*

Well, I had it ...

*(To Vital Organ)*
You know, sometimes I feel I can ... I can ... get comfortable in you. For a second. Then I get anxious. You know, troubled-like. I think ... you don't really want me there. You don't. You resist me, but you play it off.

**STAR**
*(Suggesting "not this again")*
She's driven by a kind of conditioning, friends.

**VITAL ORGAN II**
You see, I can't feel pleasure either. I can't conspire with it. It always leads me down the wrong path ... when I feel that our relationship won't be mutual—when you do the same old things you do, and brother you know what you do.

*(Concealing violence)*
Well, I just go apeshit. I go bananas.

*Audience drops to knees, enchanted. Star drops to knees, disgusted.*

*(Singing, torchy, slow)*
Love. Never spoken.
Love. Beware.
Love. Not a token.
Love. Not a dare.
(It's not a dare)
To open your heart ... to me.

*Audience moves toward Vital Organ II, but Vital Organ blocks him.*

**STAR**
*(Removed)*
She can only be stopped by applause, by the way.

*Mad Shadow's spotlit hands appear, clap, drop.*

**VITAL ORGAN**
*(Mesmerized)*
I'm not giving up my art, if that's what you mean.

*Vital Organ II draws Vital Organ to her, leads onstage. Audience turns into bench for them.*

**VITAL ORGAN II**
I would sit in your lap for hours
If you didn't ...
Fear me.

**STAR**
*(From floor, weak, attacking)*
That-a-girl, give the people what they don't really want.

**VITAL ORGAN**
*(Narcotized)*
The freshness of my—

**VITAL ORGAN II**
Talent.

**VITAL ORGAN**
The hair I let—

**VITAL ORGAN II**
Loose.
Reminds me how we were only just here, privately.

**STAR**
*(Now ancient)*
As long as we're confessing. Listen ... do you hear?

*Board enters.*

They're bored.

*White Afro and Zen Monk are handed to Star as gag props. Songbird steps forward, hands Vital Organs an X and Bird.*

They are fro-zen.

**VITAL ORGANS**
They don't know what to—

**VITAL ORGAN**
Ex—

**VITAL ORGAN II**
—peck.

*Songbird retrieves X and Bird. Star receives Bloody Decapitated Head.*

**STAR**
You are the reason we can't get a(head).

**VITAL ORGAN II**
*(To Audience, breezy)*
Hey, actor, what's wrong with this world, huh? You think you know somebody and ... wow. What about you, lover? I'm not married to him. He's just a friend.

*Songbird and Audience become dudes.*

**VITAL ORGANS**
*(Sharing lines, repeating, overlapping, sometimes laughing)*
You don't like heavy music? I do. I got into it. After my marriage. Deep Purple, I don't know.
Heavy shit like that. They were all growing their hair long. For love, right, sweetheart? Summer of love, right? You got someone?

**STAR**
*(Cynical)*
How about you, boyfriend? Show 'em how it's done? You know, bodies on the frontline type of Realness. Pip pip. Heal this big old goofy marble in the sky.
Pistols and funk doin' the talking ... until our eyes meet. And *blam*! Then ... then the world can ... ho-hum ... I can't really be bothered to finish.

**VITAL ORGANS**
*(Sickened)*
He's ... think he's ... he's thinks he's—
I don't know what he thinks ...
He thinks ...

**VITAL ORGAN II**
He's gonna win an Academy Award, that's what he thinks. I'll tell you what. He's an actor. You know what that means?

**VITAL ORGANS**
He compromises!

**STAR**
*(Hurt, insulted)*
He listens. He sees. He speaks. He feels.

**VITAL ORGANS**
Listen, sir, ma'am, hey—how do Californian gals hold their liquor? You don't know? By the ears.

*Hysterical laughter.*

Oh, I'm sick. I'm a sick, sick, human being. Ha. Ha. I'm not even a human being. Ha. Ha. Did you know that, actor? I'm not human. You played me, didn't you ... in ... what ... what were you in ... I don't know but it was a ... a superb vehicle ...

*Vital Organ spits a tooth.*

**VITAL ORGAN**
*(Stunned)*
Oh my god.

*Light shift.*

My toof.

*Star and Vital Organ II exit into audience.*

Ha. Ha. You think that was real? Ha. Ha. Country clownin' is all that is.

*Small body parts—Ears, Eyes—fall from above onto Vital Organ. Vital Organ II joins her to pick up parts.*

**CHANCE HAPPENSTANCE**
*(Offstage, talking on phone)*
Oh, okay? ... I was gonna try to make it, but I was like ... I just got so, like, tired. ... Right. ... Yeah. Right. ... Oh, that sounds great. ... Right. ... Uh-huh. ... Yeah. Right.

*Vital Organ goes dead.*

**VITAL ORGAN II**
*(Attacking)*
What the fuck did you do with my tooth?

*Star shrugs.*

You find it! You lost it, you find it!
Get on your knees, crawl!
Look for it. Get on your goddamn knees.

*Star becomes wooden puppet. Audience snaps fingers. Mad Shadow and Songbird slide to edge of stage.*

**STAR**
*(Tight-jawed, Charlie McCarthy-like)*
I'm looking, I'm looking.

**VITAL ORGAN II**
Search!

*Star wades into audience.*

**STAR**
Did you pay to get into this club? Nice shoes.

**VITAL ORGAN II**
I know what you're doing.

**STAR**
Entertaining?

*Mad Shadow gurgles, chirps.*

**VITAL ORGAN II**
Hunt!

**STAR**

*Star moves stealthily.*

Why ... what? Oh. Oh.

*Star takes tooth from Vital Organ II's hair.*

I think it may be ...
It's right here.

*Vital Organ gasps, grabs tooth, covers with kisses.*

Hurrah. And now Rabies and Middlemen, Holders of the Public Truss, Enriched Baguettes, let us once again totter down the shining path toward—

**VITAL ORGAN II**
Are you kidding?

**STAR**
Home.

*Exit Mad Shadow and Songbird, scuttling.*

**VITAL ORGAN**
*(In French)*
Something novel has transpired, something marvelous, heavenly, great!

**VITAL ORGAN II**
My body was found inside yours.

**STAR**
*(Crudely)*
Parts do turn up. You don't have my keys, do you?

**VITAL ORGAN II**
Do you know what this means?

**VITAL ORGANS**
*(Softly)*
We're bound.

**VITAL ORGAN**
My tooth, ma dent, elle est petite, oui, comme un enfant.
But she too speaks.

**VITAL ORGAN II**
She says:

*Spotlight on Tooth.*

**TOOTH**
*(Growly, possibly prerecorded)*
I am the People's vehicle, their mark and quip,
By which I mean the Menace, the deadly whip,
The lash against those for whom the boot fits,
Those thick-necked warriors of attack,
Whose rule, brother, we were sent to crack!

**STAR**
Or, "Pitbull will always be at your side."

Why do I say this?

*Mad Shadow enters in Pitbull mask. Tooth chatters.*

**VITAL ORGAN**
*(As if answering phone)*
Oh. Yes. Yes, yes, I see. Hmm-mm. Got it.

*Vital Organs move into audience, guarding and displaying.*

**VITAL ORGANS**
If this tooth hadn't flown from our mouth—why—
Actors, look at it. Touch it—why—

*(Echoing each other)*
Why, just the other day, we were talking about how it is coming, and how seriously we're at it, and that they really don't know, because if they did know, they'd object. That's right. They'd stall. All those good people doing the best they can ...

**VITAL ORGAN**
... helping, giving, loving ...

**VITAL ORGAN II**
... loving in their way ... well, the idea of one of us ... people ...

*(Singing)*
Turning up—

**VITAL ORGAN**
Armed.

**VITAL ORGAN II**
Armed!—Well, they'd rather not.

*Star gesticulates, working up audience's disgust.*

**STAR**
WE! US! Ra, ra, ra, ra, ra! WE! Le peuple, le peuple! Qui est le peuple?
Ghosts, zombies, sops. Why, the people are bagged groceries, monstrous pinups. Still lifes. The very idea sends in armed guards. Stop it. And take that horrible tooth away. It's foul. Nothing.

**VITAL ORGAN**
It comes from—Le Théâtre.

**VITAL ORGAN II**
No, from her, the Mother ... Mother Theater.

*(Livid)*
You are ... an ... opposite.

*Star laughs dismissively, and claps.*

**STAR**
Yes. And *scene*. Put that back in your heads.

**VITAL ORGANS**
Non. No.

**STAR**
Then give it to me. You're bleeding.

**VITAL ORGANS**
I know.

**STAR**
It's dangerous, friend.

**VITAL ORGAN**
Oh, it is, mon ami. Ciao.

*Exit Vital Organs. Alone, Star resorts to magic. Moves into audience, pulls tooth from someone's ear, eats it. Pulls out an eyeball, eats it. Pulls entrails up from floor, hollers, flatlines, begins theremin vocal. Stage comes alive.*

*A page of the script travels out from under curtains.*

**STAR**
What? What? And behold!

*Curtains open and close, revealing gray owl. Sound of cat meowing.*

Whoop. *Un Autre!*
Ah. With a tiny note.
Fan mail from some flounder.
Let's see ... what does it say?

*Mad Shadow leaps out to seize page, is pulled back into wings by nefarious force. Sound of truck rumbling.*

*Vital Organs appear as spotlit heads.*

**VITAL ORGAN**
You're trembling.

**STAR**
I'm cold. These actors emit a horrible frost. It bunches my nerves.

**VITAL ORGAN II**
Even pretending, you're scared.

*Star mimes pulling scroll out from Tooth.*

**STAR**
Ah, look, a movie contract! The Beast wanted to be a star after all!

How It must have suffered, Its looks being left of center 'n' all.
Poor Saint, waiting in line, rolling on casting couches
With impotent junior VPs
Wailing, emitting that foul sound
We've all come to cherish as Her music.

**VITAL ORGANS**
*(Mature, gentle, as if talking to a victim)*
I'm going to open up at some point ... and when I do I want you to know that I live beautifully. Even if you think that you are saving me with your talent, I live beautifully. Sometimes, brother, dear, pal, I hear you moaning in your hotel room at night ... it's bad. I stand there with my drink in my hand ... just rocking the ice ... just rocking the ice and listening. I hear you fall out of bed. I want to help you, but then I think—no.

**STAR**
Cut to the chase. What are you going to do with me? 'Cause I ain't going anywhere.

*Squirrel appears.*

*(Enraged)*
Not now!

**VITAL ORGAN II**
That's okay.

*(To Squirrel)*
You can stay.

*(To audience)*
Actors, nobles,
Dogs, and persons of surprising invention,
Your voice is most shrill,
Magnificent.
In a group, we can pick you out.
Therefore, you are *marked*.
Explore, as follows.

**VITAL ORGANS**
*(Echoing each other, rapid, numbed)*
There are those here tonight who, relatively speaking, have never suffered. Their pain doesn't come close to those who have been *prevented* from entering into the ranks of the Perceived, that is, the Beast,

the Beast, who knocks sense into poets, the Animal, whose wild speech, truth be told, can find no translation here. Yet actors, we sing and play in Its name, curtailing our conversations when It comes near. But I say, actors, It *is* listening tonight. It's found our den. And It is circling, because It senses blood. Not the blood of the theater but of the coursing dictum: Fight. If you cannot exchange your flesh for Its flesh, illuminating the prisons, the streets, the schools, with your glow, if you will not *become* It, if you cannot offer up your *life* without resistance, It will strike it from you. Qui est le peuple, you ask? The people carve out an existence. My body has been used as a site of pleasure, as a bag of wheat, as a source of feeling, as raw energy, but rarely have you glimpsed the depths of the love I am capable of lifting out of life. Qui est le peuple? I don't know. But I possess here the item that unites *us*: from the Mother: La Dent! The Tooth! The Bone! And I will use it to light up the world!

*Lights flourish. Songbird and Vital Organ enter as purple-wire stick figures, do "Danse Apache" to deep-bass groove as Vital Organ becomes agent of Star's demise. Star's headless body takes off Vital Organ's head. Heads dance together, return to triumphant living bodies.*

*Lights up—warm, reddish. Star trundles on, as if a woman playing a man.*

**STAR**
Here is a man trod out of light! Astonished, half awake!

**VITAL ORGAN**
*(Arms up in victory)*
Here is a woman, always the symbol of Tomorrow!

**VITAL ORGAN II**
And me!

*Star looks at Vital Organ, who looks at Star, who looks at Vital Organ, who looks at Vital Organ II, who looks at Star.*

**STAR**
*('30s chorus girl—high, squeaky)*
Madame, shall I endure such butchery,
Their thinned lips and inveterate smiles?
Look at them, not a nod!

*Ba-bum-bum-ba! All do three-quarter turn, push shoulders forward, turn heads (half snake).*

**ALL**
Say whhaaaaat?

*Enter Audience braying, then two stomps. All do locomotive, outside foot chugging.*

Hurrah! The stork is here!!
We're born again!
What a glittering success!

**AUDIENCE**
*(As himself, foppish, buffoonish, long-legged stork with fingers in his ears)*
SCREEEEEEECH!!!

*All stop.*

**VITAL ORGAN**
Actors!
Set your knives on end!
The Audience approaches at last!

*Star collapses into prayer pose.*

**STAR**
How shall we address you?

*Vital Organs collapse into prayer pose.*

**VITAL ORGAN**
As a mirror—

**VITAL ORGAN II**
As a line—

**STAR**
—as shadow of the divine?

**VITAL ORGAN**
*(To Audience, leaning in, fresh, young)*
Say, how ... how'd we do?

*Vital Organ II slaps Vital Organ's behind.*

**STAR**
*(Wet behind ears)*
Yeah, how'd we fare, pal?

*Vital Organ slaps Star. Audience draws hands up—a saint, an arbiter—beckons them to his heart, slaps them—a trick.*

**VITAL ORGAN**
*(Eyeing Audience)*
Why, he is ill.

**STAR**
*(All Andrew Wyeth's* Christina's World*)*
Very.

*Audience moseys, dances by himself.*

**VITAL ORGAN**
He looks puzzled.

**STAR**
He looks to be dazzling.

*Audience vomits, wipes mouth.*

**VITAL ORGAN II**
So empty and perfect.

*Audience lures actors toward him, drags them along.*

**STAR**
He looks to be lurching to one side.

**VITAL ORGAN**
An informant?

**STAR**
What does he tell us?

**VITAL ORGAN II**
He tells us that it will all work out in the end.

**STAR**
If we wash our hands!

**VITAL ORGAN**
Really, he says all that? He seems perfectly mute.

**STAR**
It's in his eyes.

*Audience runs and hops over all to close curtains. Greenish lighting. Music ('50s avant-garde). In front of curtains, Audience dances. Star pokes head out.*

Citizens. Shall we entertain?!

*Curtains open. All appear chorus-style with legs up.*

**ALL**
Always! More! More! More!

*Audience dances jig, will not stop hogging stage.*

**STAR**
Retreat, monster, retreat!

*Audience looks puzzled, lurches forward to choke Star.*

**VITAL ORGAN**
*(Hands to face)*
He will not.

*Audience beats Star, punching him, twisting ear, farting on head. Star is able to take a penny out of pocket, throws it to ground.*

**STAR**
Oh, look, a penny.

*Audience retrieves it.*

**VITAL ORGAN**
*(Excited, coy)*
Ah. Would there be ... a review?

*Star goes after Audience, grabs him. Throughout the following, they improvise lowbrow physical comedy.*

**STAR**
Ha! Like clockwork.

*(Pushing Audience in front of audience)*
Lesson One.

*(Showing Audience to audience)*
Here, my darling actors, is the Thing we've been waiting for, ready to be abused by your mania for attention. He is effective, ain't he? What do you think, dear Imbecile, of the following: Here is one who thinks private property ought to be abolished. He will play the role of the Youth. And here we have the Protector of the Innocents, indentured to worry. His name, for the purposes of this entertainment, is Buffet, speak it how you will, as his emotions rule him, either as a feast or as a storm that knocks about his brains. Here is the one who shall play the role of the Provocateur, friend of the rabble, demonstrator of down-worthiness, a dim reflection of a lost intellect who, once upon a time, among his betters, was left out. Ach, revenge. Mortal.

*(Turning Audience's attention to Vital Organs)*
But here, then, dear Thirster, is da Real Deal, the X-X-X-Extremist, the one against whom you, gullible and unpredictable shard of existence, shall exercise the least amount of caution, because:

*(As if delivering secret)*
She actually believes her lines.
Over to you, sisters.

*Cat-like, Vital Organs lure gullible Audience to them, grip his head.*

**VITAL ORGAN II**
Audience. Lend me your cabeza.
Look this way.

*White curtains fall. Exit Audience and Vital Organs. Music (as if in king's court—precise, stately). White curtains go up to reveal Puppets performing sweetly but stiffly, like children in a Christmas pageant. Paper Horse becomes increasingly jangled.*

**LO-PHAT**
I once saw a horse running through the desert, a horse with no rider, running fast, his nostrils flaring, his teeth on fire. No one can stop him now.

**SALAD BAR**
He'll surely die of exhaustion.

**DONKEY**
My heart hurts bad. I wanted only for him to be free.

**STARVATION**
And happy like me, in a life that knows no bounds.

*Paper Horse falters, collapses.*

**LO-PHAT**
The world is in revolt and will not stop coursing. It's running fast, faster than can be imagined. Magicians, arise, and use your old gifts!

**ALL**
Of energy!

*Lights out. Stage light on, as if post-show. Puppets are bored, confused actors.*

**LO-PHAT**
Well, that was depressing.

*(Mocking)*
What does it mean?

**SALAD BAR**
*(Airhead)*
I'm not really a political person. Well, I am but, well—

**LO-PHAT**
Not a big fan.

*(Glancing at phone)*
Hey, if we bolt, Red Lion has a happy hour, buy one get one free.

**DONKEY**
*(Innocent, disturbed)*
Like what? Drinks?

**LO-PHAT**
*(Mimicking)*
Like what? Drinks?

*Lo-Phat kicks Donkey.*

**STARVATION**
*(Adamant)*
They want to eat us. And they will eat us. Don't think for a second that doesn't include you and the food-stuffs you know and love.

**LO-PHAT**
*(Skeptical)*
Ri—ght.
Hey—!

*Lo-Phat hits Donkey.*

**DONKEY**
Ow! Why? Ow! Shit! I don't wanna die. I'm not going to jail and be locked up and go crazy and get whacked by some butt-nut.

**SALAD BAR**
He's right, I have a job, and I just started dating, and it's just, like, so much—but I don't know. I do feel like—after what my family went through—

**STARVATION**
Like standing up, Leaf?
Kale, I'm by nature a double-edged sword. I feed and I kill, so I get your ambivalence. But when the state is violently oppressive, either by neglect or direct attack, we have no choice but to respond.

**SALAD BAR**
I'm not Kale. I'm Lettuce. Why do you always have to upgrade me?

**STARVATION**
*(Noticing something)*
Look!

*Enter a series of spotlit objects: Pampers Box, Big Gulp Cup, Pizza Box, Kleenex Box.*

**ALL**
Oh, cool—

**PAMPERS BOX**
What am I doing here?

*Cup buzzes. Pizza Box emits static frequency noise. Kleenex crackles. Puppets watch until the last object leaves, then, in near darkness, form a little carousel, sing an oompah-pah song. All exit.*

*UV light. From darkness, a triptych appears, painted fluorescent with skulls, animals, and symbols of ancient power. Audience enters in hard light, half dressed, shadowed by Star.*

**AUDIENCE**
The big guy directed me to kneel
I don't remember if I complied
"Hey man," I thought to myself ... in the ... um ... 7-Eleven
And just at the very moment ... shit went down
Real fast,
Really fast,
Like everybody was nervous the guys were nervous the boys, the customers
The dude with the grin
And
Just then it was like nobody loved me, nobody cared if I lived or died so I was like
Fuck it. They were gonna take me.
You know. And I just came out
Like an animal
Like Godzilla
Pounding and wailing
I just kept like pounding and pounding and smashing
Until it was like—*fuck*—what have I done? You know.
I was like, fuck, I am still alive while this guy's ... like ... he's done.
I never met him. I didn't know the dude.
And he was ... really small.
And I thought to myself: This can't be me.
But it was.
I was in this play, watching this play,
And these people were talking about whatever
And I had this sinking feeling in my gut that
I had done this thing that was so irreversible and so unforgiveable
But at the same time, I don't know ... it seemed like it was okay too.
I just wanted to get some milk and one of those mini-burgers
You know. So I could go home.

And then all of the sudden—
I believe in invisible shields
In parallel time and stuff like that, like
Universes and places where I
Just thread space.
That's my revolution
You know what I'm saying?
Bits and pieces of me, just *(kissing sound)* deep space
I won't be here for the fight except in spirit—
On the frickin' frontlines—
See what I'm saying?
Either way, whatever goes down
I'm a victim, pure and simple
They never saw me, nobody saw me
I didn't matter
And that's why I just kept ... swinging
Where I went to ... it was like a garden.
There were heads, legitimate heads,
Like heads on pikes and heads just hanging from trees and ...
Just hanging there, you know, and I'm like whoa, you know—
What have *they* done?
What have they done to deserve this?
Even if it's quiet now and we can sleep in peace
I don't know.

*Audience pulls out folded paper. He steps forward, reads and gestures.*

I see him and I see her.
I see puppets that are like friends.
I hunger, but I don't eat.
The good I want doesn't get made.
I see actors, who nod their heads.
Their eyes shift.
Mine too.
I'm waiting and I divide the waiting into hours.
When the king died I didn't know whether to laugh or cry
But I cupped my hands for his blood.
I love my children so dearly I would make myself into a skin too, if I thought it would save them from harm.

Have I addressed everyone?

*Lights out. Deep purple light, as before starlight, fades in.*

**STAR**
I had no father but a succession of dull kings.

**VITAL ORGAN**
You had a father. You most definitely had a father.

**STAR**
*(Little boy)*
The king calls upon me, me. At night in his chamber he moves to his window, his slippers whisking the floor so as to make him like everyone else ... and then ... I don't know the word for it ... when inside his sleep ... he stares up. I feel his heart contract ... in all that power, he has ... I don't have the words for it ... and you know what? I give him the faintest pulse back. I do.

**VITAL ORGAN II**
King. King Clown.

**VITAL ORGAN**
You want to be a king ...

**STAR**
Yes.

**VITAL ORGAN**
Le père?

**STAR**
Yes.

**VITAL ORGAN II**
That means father.

**STAR**
Yes, but, sister where do you stand in all this? He asks in a high plaintive voice, wondering how much *you* make an hour? And whether a director has ever really turned on *you*?

**VITAL ORGAN II**
Never mind.

**VITAL ORGAN**
Go on.

**STAR**
When I was led to the stadium, courtyard, whatever it was ... I heard nothing ... although there were

people around me, I don't know, there were, how do you say, th-thr-throngs ... there were th-throngs, and they loved me ... I know it ... but I didn't know it at the time because, did I say, I heard nothing? I felt nothing. Only white noise, my insides throbbing against my ... insides ... I didn't feel pain ... so when the blade came, I didn't feel pain until after. T-th-th-hen I realized I used my life poorly ... I didn't ... wasn't ... anyway, I don't go in for a lot of words.

**VITAL ORGAN II**
The torturers are the ones who suffer, having to go down.

*Audience moves toward Star, holds his body like a board.*

Where their bodies are turned inside out
The palace guards wore their own viscera as shields
And burnt them on stakes
In the evening ... over and over again.

**VITAL ORGAN**
*(Listening to Star's heart)*
Their names are bitten rounds of Lorcet, Haldol, Purple ...

**ALL**
*(Whispering)*
Lorcet, Haldol ...

**VITAL ORGAN**
And the other goddesses of syrupy oblivion
Twitching at life's first instance, unstoppable now
Their nerves beat out a count till the last day.

**VITAL ORGAN II**
When the Tortured reappear
The basis of the world's great wealth
A banquet attended with such forgiveness that it strikes up horror
In men like you.

*Star breaks out of corpse-like pose. Light goes natural.*

**STAR**
Which side are you on, sister?

**VITAL ORGAN**
*(Laughs)*
I keep my business to myself.

**STAR**
That's your genius. We never know.

**AUDIENCE**
I gotta go pee.

*Exit Audience. All smile. Star leaps forward.*

**STAR**
They've made a hash of my life, hacked it to death
But don't I got it great?!

**VITAL ORGAN II**
*(Lightly singing)*
Magicians, light your lightless lamps. Put on your actor's masks.

**STAR**
There are a few things I'd like to take—

**VITAL ORGAN**
*(Singing)*
Go past the black unconscious into the deep purple night.

**STAR**
My swizzle stick from Jupiter's, my gold cuff links ...

**VITAL ORGANS**
You'll see what we have dreamt.

*Loud thump above, heavy footsteps. Star, frightened, doesn't know what to do. Decides to entertain.*

**STAR**
*(Drawing breath, then singing)*
Won't you show me, shadow,
Your hidden face?

*Star dances a soft tap, answered by footsteps above. Three taps. Three responses above.*

Your shining eyes
In the gray
Won't you let me see?
Just a moment pal
Won't you brighten?
Just for now?
Shadow, shadow, mine.

*Three taps. Three responses.*

*(Slightly emboldened)*
Revolution
Do no harm
Tap, tap, tap on my friends
Tap, tap, tap on my friends.

*Taps returned.*

Tap, tap, tap on my friends

*Star taps and stomps savagely. Boot shoots through ceiling. All cower in distress. Salad Bar comes out to see what's going on.*

But leave me behind.

*(Nervous)*
Are you there?
Little wolf. Are you there?

**BOOT**
*(Deep bass)*
Not quite, mon frère, not there.

**VITAL ORGAN**
*(Softly)*
When will you come, little Loup ...

**VITAL ORGAN II**
Will you come all the way through?

**BOOT**
Not yet, ma petite soeur
Ce n'est pas encore l'heure.
But I will, little one, I will come.

*All back away.*

**STAR**
Are you wild, Mister Wolf?
Are you tame?

**VITAL ORGAN**
Will you tell us, Monsieur Loup?

**VITAL ORGAN II**
What's your name?

**BOOT**
No. But let me sing

*(Singing, discordant)*
Mother, you did wrong
Left me for so long.
Now I don't know you.
Or was it me who bailed?
Who cares?

*(Spoken)*
How sad it is my job to hurt you
Well, let your devastation be your art.

*Exit Boot. Light goes deep blue-purple.*

**STAR**
*(Confessing)*
Moments ago, the lights came up and you saw me here
You waited for me to triumph.
Like morphine,
You waited for the effect of my presence
By stepping out here
I promised as much
But my presence slips through you.

**VITAL ORGAN**
That old Star? Stage actor?
The child-man who never knew.

**VITAL ORGAN II**
Just how closely his father followed him
Whose eyes remained moist, always ...

**VITAL ORGAN**
Even licking an envelope, he'd kind of
Well up.

**VITAL ORGAN II**
He too steps forward and with his violent indifference says:

**STAR**
Isn't it enough to know that I am leaving?
Like all actors
I am leaving the world again and what a pleasure it is!

Not to have to work everything by hand
Look what came of it: the doorknob.
Never found outrage in my teeth
Only in my skin, which remains warm, calm, and attached to the bone.

**VITAL ORGAN**
The woman artist suffers ridicule—

**VITAL ORGAN II**
Although her warnings are often right.

**STAR**
I wish you wouldn't continue, dear.

**VITAL ORGANS**
*(Lightly)*
Sir, you are a wonderful—

**STAR**
Thank you!

*(French accent)*
Revolution is a rich man's game
Full of old-timey words and shadowboxing
Down my side of the street, the killing is everyday
Ain't that right, ladies?
It's all soda fountains and wine bars for them
Bus stops and bust-ups for us
But we'll travel along, won't we?
We'll be—under the boards, looking up skirts and taking numbers
While dey writing papers, we're kiting checks
You know what, actors? I think I love you
Your visages are very sweet, very kind.

*Star retreats as hands form corona around his spotlit head. A hand curls around Star's forehead to pull him—protesting—into darkness.*

The moment the skin responds, the surface vessels burst ... the veins are like rays. They reach—out—marvelous ... !
Shockproof the theater, I say,
Keep all the jolts away!

*Vital Organs own stage. They dance, meow, scratch floor, hang on curtains.*

**VITAL ORGAN**
*(To audience)*
Hey Big Girl with the Skinny Heart, Beast Rida, I'll miss ya.
I'll miss your mind-rape, your numbness, your lack of applause.

**VITAL ORGAN II**
I'll miss the hard self-hatred across every young girl's brow, and all the nasty, dirty sex, plastic film, and the feeling that whatever happens, there'll be a comeback.

**VITAL ORGANS**
Toot, toot, and blow your own horn.

**VITAL ORGAN II**
Blow it across the sea now for the ham-fisted Giant's going home. Countrymen? Shall we bring down the house? Shall we finally use our teeth?

*Enter Donkey. Music (pop metal).*

**DONKEY**
*(Singing, earnest, Prog-ish)*
When you die every day
And no one sees your pain
You get right mad

*Midsong, Vital Organs grab Donkey and toss him back and forth. Popcorn spills everywhere. They begin to violently kill Donkey, as Mother Theater's Mouth opens. Her long tongue enters, flopping over them to lick the audience. Exit Vital Organs, fighting or running. Tongue rises upward in victory, shrivels off.*

Or you retreat
When they put you down
You go deeper in the ground
Nobody to lift you
On your feet

Oh love, oh, love
Oh love we are the fools
Oh, love oh love—
Oh love
The world it turns
Just for me.

*Disco curtain call.*

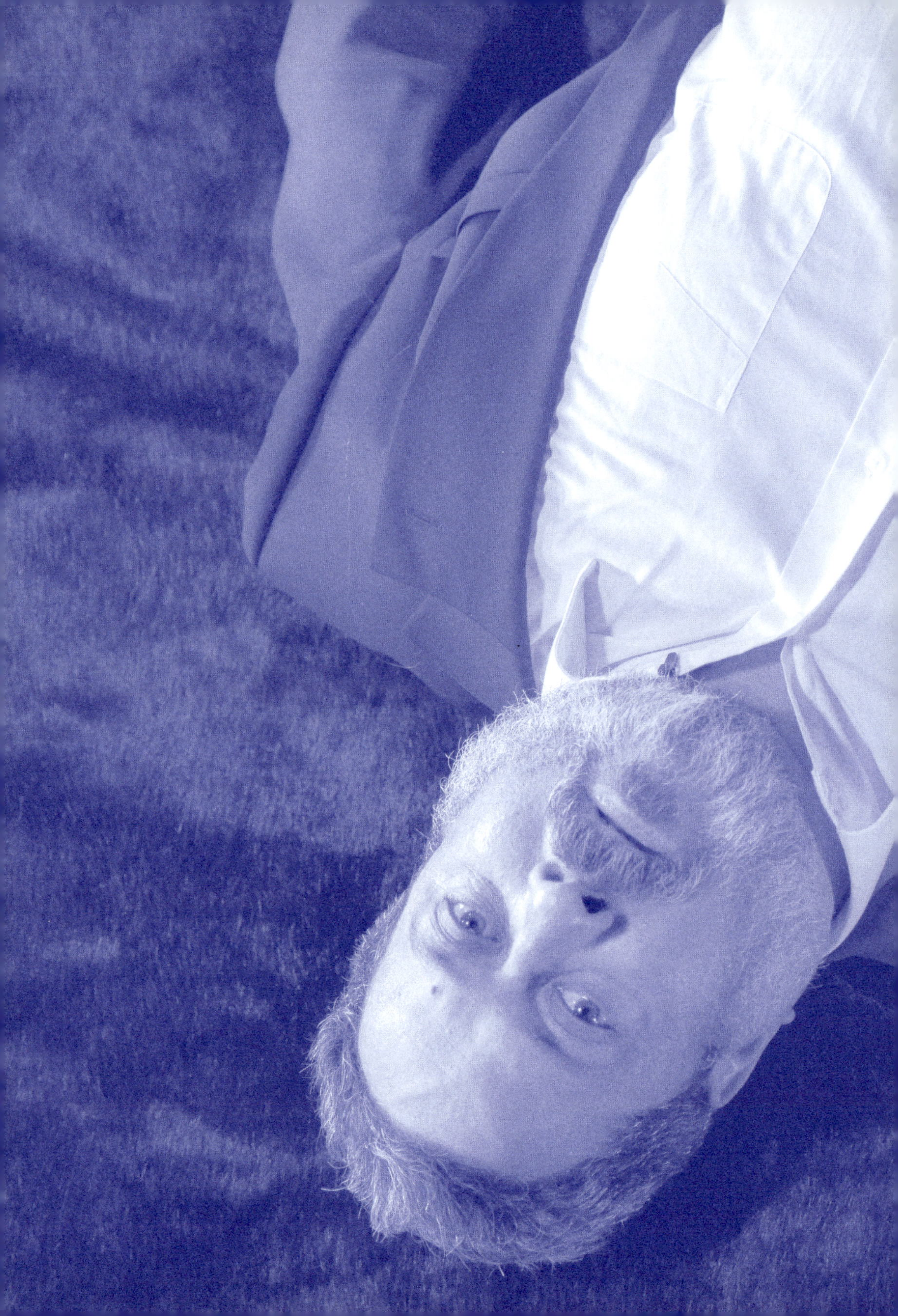

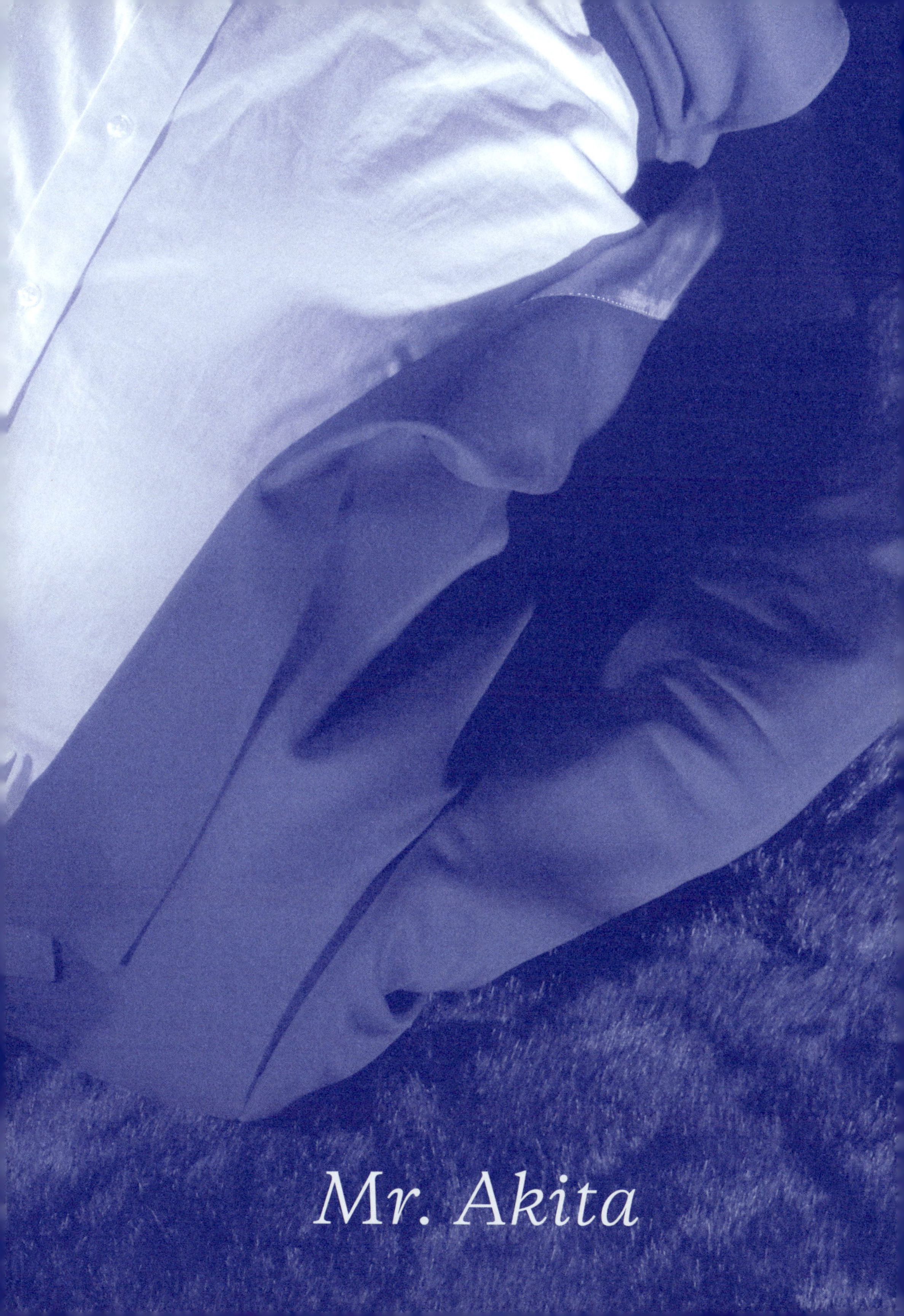

# Mr. Akita

Written and directed by Asher Hartman

First performed at the Tang Teaching Museum, Skidmore College, Saratoga Springs, New York, September 26, 2015, as part of the exhibition *Machine Project: The Platinum Collection (live by special request)*

MAN . . . . . . . . . . . . . . . . . . . . . . . . . . . . . . . . . . . . . . . . . Cliff Hengst
PAINTING . . . . . . . . . . . . . . . . . . . . . . . . . . . . *Sun Burn (Split) 1* by Emily Joyce

*Enter Man in a suit. He will be a Borscht Belt comedian, de Kooning, a watery ghost, a painting, Christ/Jack Nicholson. Stage directions are often spoken. Those that are not appear to the left.*

**MAN**
It's fall, and I'm feeling repose, not tough any more like I was used to.
I'm moribund, but in a good way.

*Elegant now, cocked head, posing.*

There are December days
I won't miss ...
Stars aligning. Nah. Not really.
Not me.

Not me
Was poor like you
Born tired like you
With
Liberty
Smarts
And a black blazer
On fire
Hell-bent and held back
Angelic-like,
Tiptoeing
I made my way into the land of suits and big money
Scratch, green, moola, doll bait, devil's arugula, chedda, ducats, stacks, slosh, cake, nose whistle, da bidness, payday, Bennie's laundry, the beat, mummy's moisturizer. What for?
For this I've driven myself over the world and back?
For the banks? The old good boys, the dreamers, the hunks?
If you say so.
I'll trust ya.

Cadillacs? 'Member them?

*Awareness.*

I ... uh ... wow, I'm outta here ain't I? ... I—

*Dreamy, soft, realizing, sings softly, "Spill the wine, take that pearl"*

*In front of every kind of girl ...*
*There was long ones, tall ones ...*

*He sees the Painting,* Sun Burn, *from across the room.*

Look at that picture.

Who d'ya think's behind that?
Some mustachioed man? Grave robber? Some con artist?

No. A yoot, a yoot ... someone whose eyes flutter in the light, someone for whom a ciggie butt is the first transgression, someone who wants his parents dead, 'n' loves them so much he calculates to the second just how old he'll be when they're plugged and buried.

*High voice, whiny.*

"It w-w-w-on't hurt at fifty." Wrong. It always hurts. Life hurts. Know that.

*Picking up the phone.*

Hey, Mom!—Oh. Right.

How she used to be: the curve of her side, carving the air, over and over, your all, your nothing, your light. I remember the sun catching the strands of her hair when she'd lean over ...

Now that she's *a was*, there's no—

*Glancing at the Painting.*

radiance.

So the youth practices, rehearses in the valley of the dead 'n' gone, in painting class, intermediate, along the rough geometry of bottles and cans, vases set up by the old prof, a wheezer with rims who hasn't seen his dick in a decade let alone a good bag of weed, things you can use, ya know. No, he knows nothing of that ... hey ... come to think of it—he knows only—space.

*And now there is a long space. Not a pause, but space.*

You over there in the sunlight! So far from me, Artist ... whatcha doing? Dreaming of docks? He-men who could break you in two, gorillas with you flat overhead like a stick, like this. Why, they would smash you if you weren't so damn pretty. You got talent. Know what I mean? Talent. I'll let you go. Go on! Make sense of your life. Go! Get outta here! Run! Before I put you in soup.

The youth, subtle, eyelashes curved upward like a baby's, the jaw imperceptibly slack, so full of wonder ... confidence.

Hey, Artist, show us how lame and broken we are. Huh? How 'bout it? Hey! Don't run away like that! I'm talking to you! Hey!

Our insides. Petrified.

*Inhales.* Waiting for the verdict.

Teachers: are they a) shot to bits, b) curled into balls, c) robot rabbits with yellow teeth dripping bile, d) all three?

Without them we plod along, cafeteria-style, waiting for something we can talk about.

*Duh. Bucktoothed.* "Hey, did you notice how the needle hit the record?"

Nope, said the Artist. I refuse. Nothing in mind just then, really, but whether he used too much blue.

*Jerry Lewis-style. "Duh."* Maybe the pitcha should hang another way, huh, what d'ya think? Is that how it 'posed to be?

Huh? Huh?

*Beat. De Kooning speaks.* "Where is our salvation? Certainly not in your musings, your short autobiography," teacher used to say to me, the Painter. I saw holograms around him, Thai stick and coffee cans, dancing, rotating, like sprites. His hair matted, he used to say: "So your sister drowned? Write it down. I guarantee you in fifty years you won't remember her face. Late night, opening a can of corn, the blade half in, suddenly you'll feel a chill. 'Who's there? Who goes?' You turn around, partially, failing to recognize her image as it flashes against the cupboards, her one appearance a sunburn, scorching your retina, then gone."

*Wait, what?*

"Your dog ran away? Now that's a tragedy. That makes me cry," teacher said, lowering that Styrofoam cup for once.

"All that life, like a firecracker ... he had so much anger, that dog. He wanted to be free, buddy. Feel me? He wanted to be arm in arm with endless soda, free snacks—"

*Snapping his fingers.* "—chicks. Now he only knows bloat and the throbbing of his own muzzle, the routine."

*Dully plodding.* *Clip clop clip clop clip clop ...*

My art teacher was a dog with a curled tail. Used to give assignments. "Tear limbs," he'd say. "Develop an eye, a look, a stare, work on the sneer of a wannabe, someone who coulda but wouldna." He shook his head.

Mr. Akita, that's him. He once thought in an airport, turning around from the baggage claim, "Good God, I see it all. I see it. The way it works. Everything! Everything! Now if I could just get this down on ... a napkin." Then, just as suddenly, "Hey, look, barbeque potato chips, free, if you fill out this survey. Wow."

His mind wanders.

Painting versus Tree. Round one. Tree has friends. Painting has hangers-on.

*As the Painting, breathy.* "Dear ones, if there was some way I could communicate to you the depth of my refinement without losing your attention," the Painting says.

The hangers-on check their phones.

*He walks upstage.* He gets up here to entertain.

Backless, he takes a risk, showing the trail, the whole shebang from neck to the crack, the death drop. But wait—there's more:

*Crouched, then swerve, rock the head.* How might I humbly serve? Gimme all your money, you newbies! Desire, oh, that's what I want. I want your need. Your gotta!

*Sings.* *Spill the wine, take that pearl.*
*Spill the wine, take that pearl.*

*He creeps toward the audience.*

I was prowling when I felt your need, and I just snatched it. I took it home and I was like, bitch, sit down, and your need says, like hell I will, ball boy, and I said, bitch, I'm gonna slap you back to the day you dropped your candy and your daddy laughed.

Your need got real quiet. I hitched up my belt and smiled. Gotcha. Says I, and went to bed. Well. It weren't but at around midnight when your need got up. Got a rope, see, and a bucket of water, looked around, needy eyes shifting back and forth, pulled back the curtain, determined that it would shrink me; it would husk and strip and soak me in that little bucket until I came out nine inches tall. But I saw it standing over me. With one eye, I peeped and saw your need with that rope, and I said, "Need, you bore me. You're worse than an old episode of *Columbo*." "That's where you're wrong, Columbo. I couldn't have possibly killed you. I was in rehearsal that night, for my play, a play about your demise. It's called *You Don't Care About Much, Do You?* So you see, so I couldn't have possibly killed you, because I was in fact murdering you, and that's quite a different thing." Columbo scratches his head. "Well, you got me, sir. You got me. I hate to admit it, but you really got me."

Ah, sweet museum, liar, calculating bastard. Art is a liar. For sure, for sure. The province of the not-like-you.

Feed the paintings apples. They enjoy it. They long to be like us, but not too fat. "Where's the balance of girth against greatness?" They cry, shrilly. "What does a human being have to do to be just right?"

*And now a delicate Jacques Tati-inspired move where I lift this building over my head and break it like a bone. Everyone in it. We're all relics now. Just like that. Snap.*

Mr. Akita, my art teacher, lived with the Hamburglar. He had no choice. He knocked the Hamburglar up. And now it was a done deal.

"I'm stiff with you, Hamburglar," he'd say in one of his late-night fits. "You are not current. You do not float my boat. You are POOOOOOR!, Hamburglar, and that's your essential fuck-up. You have no say. You are wanted by the police. Click here for details."

The Hamburglar, like the Romano cheese, like that pair of nasty underwear grilling on the heater, like the remains of a steak sandwich in an Arby's wrapper, and the broken printer, said nothing.

The Painting, however, spoke.

"Ah, yes, gently, the Painting dips a cookie, takes it to its lips."

*Gingerly crossing to the Painting.*

"You work with your hands, I see," said the Painting.

*The Painting nibbles the cookie's edge.*

No shame in that, says I, working with your hands, like a laborer—

*Pesci-style.*

—except you're not, are you? You don't labor. You sit around all day toying with your prick, cashing your gramma's checks, running out with your girlfriend to buy shit, Jeno's Pizza Rolls. You're not a laborer, you're a cheat. You wanna fuck with the memory of a dead woman? You'll never know the depths of what she felt looking at you in that fucking cradle, the meals she missed so you could gobble down whirled peas, and now you're buying shit pizza with your side piece on that woman's legacy? You're not an artist; you're a kid, dreaming. Cut it out.

*He breathes, heavily, insulted, on* fire.

Mr. Akita ran ... wildly, out onto the tundra, his tongue shred by incisors so fine they tore ribbons, ribbons of meaty pink, sea green, swamp yellow, fecal gray ... he let his pride unfurl behind him, surprised and embarrassed at the delicacy of his paws, the marks left in the white plains, the snow, as it vanished behind him.

"Goodbye to all things life has to offer! So long!" quoth he, fleeing.

*He fake-pants heavily.*

"It's over, isn't it?" The dog panted at the tip of the ice island. "I'm out. Outties. Outta here. Donies. Done."

"Ah, no, Mr. Akita. I think you gotta lil bit of gumption in you yet," you say, snickering into your cupped palm.

"Why was I given life? Why did I come here if not to take all?!" Akita cries.

*He approaches the Painting.*

"Dear Vortex, what have you to offer me? Where are my thunderstorms, my black clouds, darting birds that peck the eyes? Dear Painting," said my teacher, his eyes rimmed red, his breath a crystallized ointment for an unspeakable disease. He let his hand track the surface. "Dear Painting, I am better than my father, aren't I? Please say yes."

*Light, the Painting, sputters.*

The building crushes the man.

Dear Painting. You didn't ask to be born. Evidence of someone else's existence, made to stand for it without consent. Victim of a thumb and a forefinger. You sorry fuck.

*Sings.*

"Grandma's hands used to churn the homemade butter ... "

Painting, you embarrass me. You tell the world I wanted to be heard.

*A classmate fishes:*

"Well, maybe if you made it a little more obvious; maybe if you told us what it was about."

*Silence. Rest.*

"Grandma's hands clapped in church on Sunday morning."

Teacher told me about his wife, his girlfriend, his ex-girlfriend, his ex-ex-girlfriend, a couple of guys he knew who didn't make it after the war.

"Ah," he said, scuffing the ground with his low, brown heel. "Shit."

Coral sands
Pink sands
Amber sands
Golden sands
Drifting sands ...

The dog stands at the edge of the highway, a Navajo sunset before his bent silhouette. Ah. That plague, Desire.

"I can't even talk to my man," your drowned sister said to me, when she returned from one of her haunts. "He has no head space for me. After I drowned, it was like I never existed."

"Yeah?" I said. "Well. Maybe if you explained ... "

"Forget it," she said, fading from the venetian blinds.

Amber sands. Coral sands. Pink sands. Golden sands. Then aqua.

You'll never know.

*Jack Nicholson uses her ghost, egregiously:*

What I'm trying to capture here is how there are so many thought-spores, we have no way to communicate except in pitchers that compress them. Ideograms above Christ's head. That eye—G-money—watching you. Dear Painting, how did you know what I was thinking that? Goddamn.

Get something in the mouth
Real fast.
Push it in. Tunnel of love, the kisser.
When you love a person, you eat that person.
Head first
Even the bones

All of it
Goes in.

"So, uh, what about you and me?" I asked my teacher,
Mr. Akita, kinda nervous at first.

"The hysterical man soils himself.
Repercussions are immediate.
Back to boyhood!
Look that monster in the eye, kid!
Tear it up!"

I noticed a small amount of poison on Akita's lips.
A dot of the sizzurp, spreading fast, a thick layer of
that sweet cherry, thinning.
Between number one and number two.

The student deadens himself to avoid getting hopped
up on the old prof's broken cart. But inside, his rib
cage is exaggerated to contain the bigger heart.
Cause of death, I'd say.

Two paintings walked into a bar.
The first said, Gimme a thrill.
The other said, Gimme all your money, your life, your
mind, your would-be children, your hope against
hope; your self-esteem; your crouching, servile
sense of time; the ability to orient yourself in space,
the knowledge that you've soiled your adult diapers,
you don't have much time left, and you didn't make
the grade.
Bartender says:
See the hole in the back of this bar?
And the paintings looked and saw the coral
sands, the ochre sands ... the golden sands ...
and the aqua ...
Pure silence.

*Lunging forward and back.*

Mr. Akita paints by the cabin door
Like Pollock but meaner, less ambitious
Eyes narrowed, forehead creased
You see the belly of his forest-green corduroy shirt
Come in and out of the slice
Between lintel and post
Headphones on like '97
Folgers on board
Brewing.

And there he is, suddenly, in the passenger side of your vehicle
Not surprising really
He's been there so many times, but not entirely visible
You keep your mouth shut.
Turn the radio up.
After a while you say what you've rehearsed:
"Where ya going?"
Dog's black tongue hangs to one side, the glistening saliva gathers at the base of a nicotine-stained tooth.
"Oh yeah," you say, "I was thinking about going that way too."
You detect that his eyes have widened, slightly
Maybe he knows this is bullshit.
"Whatever," you say to yourself. "I don't care about this old fool."
You change the station.

Santana comes on.

*" ... Jean and Joan and a who knows who ...*
*I'm getting tired ... of ... feel ... feel ... like ... a fool ...*
*My house is dark ... pots are ... cold."*

Mr. Akita's eyes widen, this time for real.
"Do you believe in angels?" he says.
"Uh." You're not sure where he's going with this.
"Uh."

He may be your angel, though, you think, as you survey his chest, like the curve of your mother's hips, proud, lifted, the red, rough coat alluding to the cottony, vulnerable fur beneath, the heart, the beating muscle, pounding hard.
"Yes," you say, certain now.
"Yes, I do." He is your angel, your pal.
"Mmph," he says, a streak of cactus and tumbleweed registering behind him.

"Jupiter," says Mr. Akita at the campfire after you've made love.

*Jerry Lewis.*

"Jupiter is the most largest, most streaky colored planet you'll find."

God, this dog is dumb, you realize now, nodding.
"Oh?"
"Yeah," he says, "Pretty much. I guess there's others, though, prolly."
"Wow."
"Mm-hmm."
"Like a Rothko?"
"No, more streaky."
"De Kooning?"
The conversation tapers.
"Is there any more beans?" he finally says, nudging the can with his muzzle.

Maybe there's a code in all this, maybe like if you break down the numerical value of each letter of what you say, something parts in the sky, like a realization of why you're here and what you were born to do. You'd see that it's all in the plan, everything, all those years of sleeping in, the hit-and-run at your uncle's farm, the death of that cat, the years of changing jobs, looking through rock formations, drinking all that Diet Coke; the change of looks: beard, no beard, gay, not gay, bi; all those white slips on the table, Wendy's four dollars and four cents, Taco Bell, three dollars and eleven cents, Mr. Coffee, seven dollars and eighteen cents, if you add it all up, you get the number 14.69, which reduces to the number four, which is DEATH, no, to number 2, which is LOVE

4.4
3.11
7.18

Don't let the animal in, not the real animal.

*Walks ghost-like across the split in the audience.*

*About the aura.*

I'll deny it. I'll deny that it's here, here in this room. I'll become very still. We'll sit side by side, neither of us moving. To move would be an admission of belief that we are both here. A movement assigns space territory. *Sssh*. Dare not. Dare not enter.

The animal comes in on his belly.

*Nasal, tense, Jack Nicholson reads from a book:*

"I'll show you a bit of the wound," Christ said. "The drip. A hint of where it went wrong, but not all. For that, O Painting, would be to boast. No, Father, I think I sorta redeemed myself on this one, don't you think?"

*Clouds, unchanged above.*

"Well I liked it anyway."

"All the other kids drew their trees firmly planted in the ground. Now me. I knew better," said Christ. "I knew that's not the way it was."

Banality as threat. Oh, you never heard that?

Americans, with our nasal can-do attitude, muffin tops, closed lips, disinterest as rebellion, Hulk miniatures stuffed headfirst in the gravel, porousness, ache, and no answer to the rifle on repeat. Nada. How we make our art. Certain. That's how we like it. Certain. The curator's soft nod, thinking about all the things that she shouldn't have said in the prelude to the artist's lecture. "What's he talking about, anyway? This guy's a pretender. Who is he fucking? Oh, I know."

"What is life but violation and recovery?" Mr. Akita asked, flippantly, his nose whistling. I saw him in the grocery store one last time. With some student irritated that he had to pass his hand over every jar of peanut butter and jelly in the aisle: jelly alone, jam alone, peanut butter alone, creamy, chunky, salted, unsalted, organic, and crap; peanut butter and jelly interlaced, intertwined, interlarded, as it were. He had to feel the hard glass against his palm to know he was still in it, still in the game.

I spoke to him, looking at the ground, then to the oranges, to the fresh un-shucked corn.

"Sorry, I couldn't take your class. I had some ... refurbishing ... my grandmother ... twisted ankle ... hives ... " I mumbled.

That night he raped me.

His mouth opened around me like the hood of an old Pontiac. The stink of Marlboros, asada, and that fresh un-shucked corn. Blackness overtook me. I stayed in his belly like a fetus, sunk to his groin. Time became sips of breath. When he stood, I felt sick. I could feel my own weight sag at the end of his end. I could feel the burden I became when he got up to pee or when he checked the mail. I could hear the shush shush shush of his slippers, and when he raised his hand to the canvas with that brush like a claw, I felt the sick of a newborn who knows there ain't nothing more to it than this.

*I adore you, Painting!!! You're better than life. You're an imitation of it!!!!!*

You pass! Forests, rivers, lice, they give me the creeps. They don't acknowledge me like you do. You're real! I love you!!!!!!!!!!!!

*The Painting sputters.*

"You old witch," I say, hanging on to the tilt of my professor's pubis. "You junkie, you seahorn!"

Sufferer like me, Painting, your music is an infinimare, a never-ending siren's call into that blank sublime, white, white like the desert, the camera flare, a hundred sea dogs' heads in the afterimage you call up. I hate you!

You took my heart and tossed it into that hole ... that at the end of the day ... at the end of the day, at the end of the day, when you add it all up, it's self-pity that put me to sleep in this old man's gut. I lay there in his stink.

Sigh.

Your teeth, Painting, Demoiselles' hurtful remarks, African can openers, fierce, fierce tears, fringed light.

The Painting's retort:
"Viewer, you can never know."

*Phone fingers.*

No.
Yes.
Ah. What time?
No. That won't work for me.
No. No, not at all.

That will not work for me at all.

The Painting's wound spreads, sun-like.

Teacher says:
What is a sun?
Can anyone tell me?
Can anyone tell me?
Yes? Akita?

*"A sun is the object that rages back."*

"Well, that's not quite right," teacher says.
"But you're very close."

*End.*

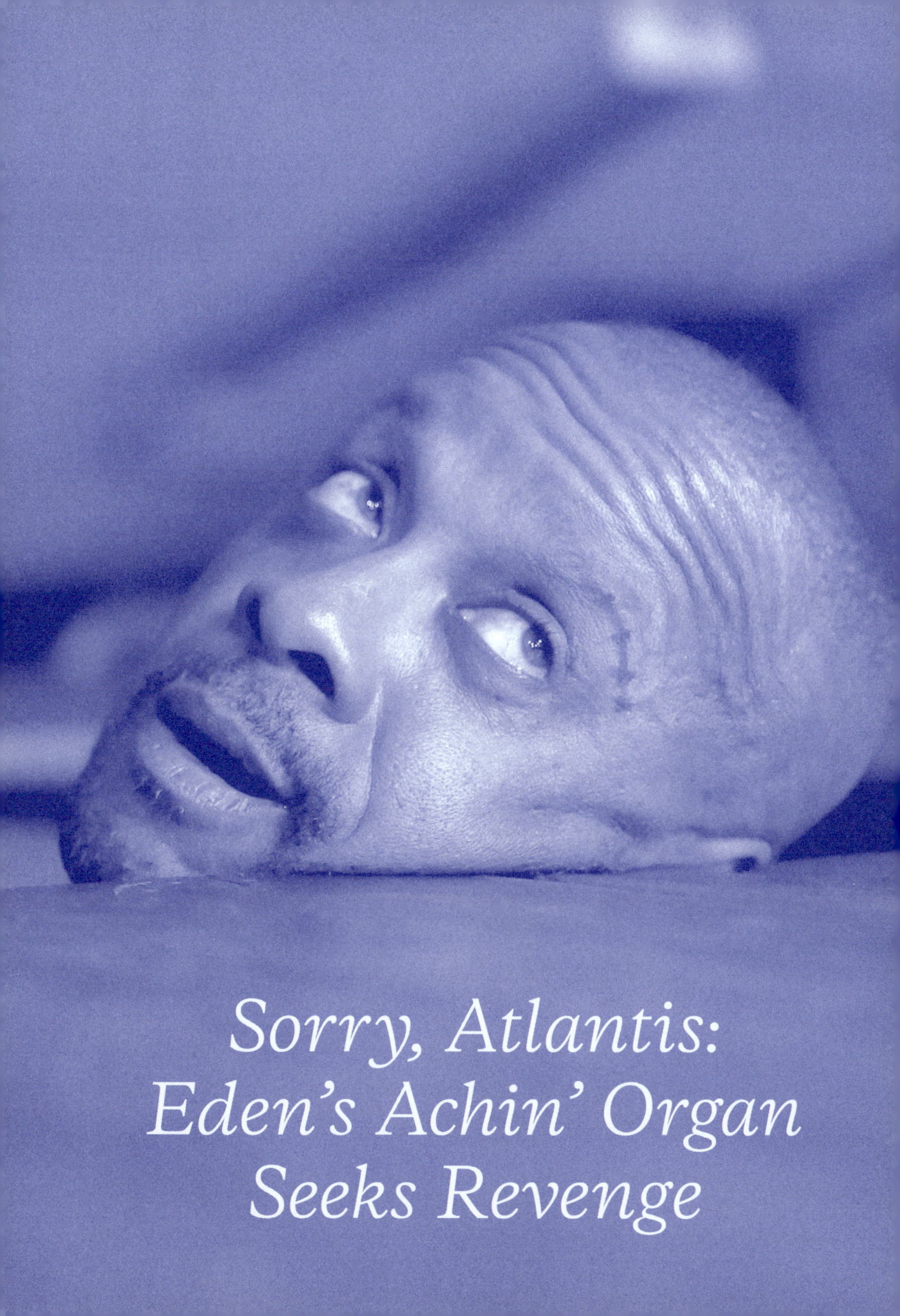

# *Sorry, Atlantis: Eden's Achin' Organ Seeks Revenge*

Written and directed by Asher Hartman

First performed at Machine Project, Los Angeles, September 21, 2017
Assistant Director: Tim Reid

SLEDGEWEED, a snail, full-figured . . . . . . . . . . . . . . . . . . . . . . . . . . . . . Zut Lorz

POJO, lizard twins with enormous stuffed phalli . . . . . . . . Paul Outlaw and Joe Seely

HARRY WHO TOMATO FACE, a psyclops, Hades, a soldier . . . . . . . . Michael Bonnabel

FREEBIRD, Satan, redheaded . . . . . . . . . . . . . . . . . . . . . . . . . . Chelsea Rector

POSEIDON, a god / HAIRY HAIRY WOMAN, mother of POJO . . . . . . . . . . . Philip Littell

CLOUDS, six judges . . . . . . . . . . . . . . . . . . . . . . . . . . . . . . balcony audience

RABBLE . . . . . . . . . . . . . . . . . . . . . . . . . . . . . . . . . . . . . . . lower audience

OLD SPLINTERS . . . . . . . . . . . . . . . . . . . . . . . . . . . . . . . . . . . . . . the stage

FOUR SHADES, in soft bathing caps . . . . . . . . . . . . . Chelsea Rector, Philip Littell,
Michael Bonnabel, and Joe Seely

PUPPETS CHORUS: PEASEASHIT, a worried piece of shit; Harry's mangled limbs (GRIZZLED WHITE LEG, ARM PIECE WITH TANTALIZED FINGERS); FRECKLED FLOPPY WHITE FISH; Freebird's FOUL PUPPET BIRD, a.k.a. FOUL BIRD; golden WEEDS; three ENCHANTING FISH; STYROFOAM CUP; WORMS; FLEETING BEINGS, glowing orbs; BLADE OF GRASS; long, soft GOLDEN TUBE stuffed with Brawny paper towels; three DOLPHINS

*Cut into a wooden raked stage are six holes—round and square, some with trapdoors—surrounding a big hole that serves as a hot tub, a pond, and an entry to the underworld. Two audiences sit before the stage: at balcony level, six judges in white wigs; below, rabble on benches above a grated floor. Actors will play to both, but most decidedly to the judges.*

**ACT I.** *I smell your teeth, Mudder*
**Scene 1.** *Dawn.*

*Ocean smell. Darkness, then blue light of dawn. Sounds of flies buzzing, waves, seagulls.*

*A hand with cowbell rises from central hole. Ding-ding-ding! PoJo pop up from rectangular holes. A spray of ocean water issues from Jo's mouth.*

**JO**
*(Pleading)*
Oh Clouds, Clouds, ye knows our fates
M'izer loves a pal, drunk on ig'nance
And we two, Brudda, dopes in the grind.

**PO**
*(Innocent)*
Know nuttin', nuttin'.

**JO**
Shot clean outta stars—
Twins, friends, we plopped in da stew
Candidates for a land's end,
Where da hard edge meets da blue
Say, Brudda, how's 'bout a smile?

*Po pouts, issues squeak.*

Smile or I'll clap youse!

*Po smiles as if he doesn't know how to work his mouth.*

*(Threateningly)*
Oh, you great flycatcher, you insult me with your wisp.
Put on a big one!

*Jo mimes punching Po, who teeters. Ding-ding-ding!*

**PO**
I culd like to have a pig for a pet and take care of 'im.

**JO**
*(Too cute)*
Wud you love 'im?

**PO**
Oh, yes.

**JO**
Say, here comes ol' Slimeball, uninvited. Hide!

*A pair of hands feels around the edges of a hole. Sledgeweed rises—joyful, smiling. PoJo duck.*

**SLEDGEWEED**
La, la-la-la, la, la, la!
Say, dirty woild,
Say!

*Flute plays (effervescent).*

How refreshin' ta hear a melody 'gainst the gods dat wore us out
Wonders me how dey run and if dey eva looked back.

*(Looking back, tricky)*
Ah, death, death of all beliefs, where dat next step may be took?
Ha ha ha ha. Gods, ah, good luck, dey run away.

*Sledgeweed spreads arms, falls face-forward.*

Say, ol' Plank dat holds us up above da Drink?

*Wood-creaking sound as Sledgeweed scoots upstage.*

Ol' Splinters, how goes? Keep us from da Deep, will ya, from all lasting quiet ...

Now dese two!

*Sound of fingernail underneath Old Splinters—long.*

Easy puddins.
Are youse down dere?

*Sound of strange winds, bass flute. All make windmill arms. PoJo's bodies shake.*

**PO**
*(Hiding, giggling)*
Nope, nobody home.

*Sledgeweed scoots along, makes baby tawk.*

**SLEDGEWEED**
Wouldn't I see if I had eyes?

Here come da protons, da splittin' winds.

*She cups her bosom, looks into her décolletage, pokes out lower lip.*

Clouds dere is strange. Tings are like today and yet tamara. How can I say?
Dere's a gap.

*Peaseashit rises.*

**PEASEASHIT**
Greasy time, it slips, friend. No rescue.

*Peaseashit exits. Smell of cologne and garbage.*

**SLEDGEWEED**
Where had dat gap gone, Peaseashit?

*Sledgeweed plugs nose, fans air, exits.*

Ah, an ol' my gud'ness! Comes a ranklin' smell!

**PO**
*(Sexy)*
Ah. All squalls and light. Sears me eyes. Come, disgrace me.

*Jo pushes Po to the wall, slaps him, fucks him. Sea shanty plays. Harry's mangled limbs and Freckled Floppy White Fish bobble and play.*

*Freebird rises with Arm Piece With Tantalized Fingers.*

**FREEBIRD**
*(Taunting)*
Yet how many did da sea wit its wet tongue flick?

Bob bob bob kick kick kick right'chere?

*Hard cowbell: Clang-clang!*

Lookie here! Ahoy!

*Harry Who Tomato Face appears rising and falling in the big hole. He's in tatters—military braids torn apart, jacket bitten and bloodied.*

**HARRY**
Oh-kay, oh-okay-o-okay, oh, okay-now, brudda. We're jus' passing tru.

*Sledgeweed pops up, nostrils plugged with toilet paper.*

**SLEDGEWEED**
*(Snickering)*
Caught in da brine, eh?

**HARRY**
All right, all right. We're just passin' tru, let us pass.

*Exit Leg, Fingers, and Fish.*

**FREEBIRD**
Chop chop!

*Exit Sledgeweed and Freebird, laughing.*

**SLEDGEWEED**
Get a leg on!

**POJO**
*(Pounding stage)*
War's over, pal, scram!

*Harry slides toward PoJo, palms cupped.*

**HARRY**
Nuttin' for da lost cause?

**POJO**
Scram, soldier! You heard our mouths!

**HARRY**
Well, I won't be the last stab!

*Repulsed by Harry's smell, Jo vomits in hole.*

But here's the news, fellas: You killed and killed again, but your knives retract. What you killed with confidence, once again, comes back.

*Sound of hammer below.*

**POJO**
Hey! Say what you mean, Bits 'n' Pieces!

*Po runs to vomit.*

**HARRY**
Well. Now. You've had your clang. I've rung your little bell. Alas ... I must be traveling on.

*Harry slithers into hole.*

**PO**
Look at his lips, curved wit' pleasure at keepin' us out.
Well, here's da ting—dead men don't rise!

**JO**
*(Arch)*
Dey seems very dead when you last sees 'em!

*Three frog croaks. Enchanting Fish rise, then Sledgeweed—beautiful and confident. Ribet-ribet-ribet. PoJo look down, at each other, then down.*

**ACT I. Scene 2.** *Oh, yes, Brudda*

*PoJo fist bump, smile.*

**POJO**
Oh, yes, Brudda, boys will love.

*Arpeggio as Sledgeweed slides up, smiling.*

**SLEDGEWEED**
Who's the cream of the crop?

*PoJo fall to their bellies. Sledgeweed plops into a hole. PoJo lick other holes, giving Sledgeweed pleasure. Synth carousel music (distorted, strange). PoJo prepare dicks to fuck holes—salting and peppering, spitting. Sledgeweed bounces in the center hole, bored. Pulls out "Pennysaver" paper, becomes absorbed in bargains. PoJo cum loudly, collapse. Exit Sledgeweed. PoJo rock back and forth, lazily kiss.*

**PO**
Don't go up dere nasty!

**JO**
"I-won-u-do-me," sed da corner hoo-er or what we used to call big Fattie.
Don't know what she had in dat pooch, but it weren't hue-man.

**PO**
Ooh, drop dat lick, drop dat lick, drop it down on my fleshy gun.
Oh, big Fattie, big, I love youse.

*A-note on synth. Sledgeweed rises to stand, showgirl-like.*

**SLEDGEWEED**
*(Singing, delicate, off-key)*
Now is the time for da sex organs to turn to gold. The feeling state is the loving state, how, how, how, how, how, how, is it possible to looooooove!

*Worms and Weeds dance beneath her. She waves goodbye, jumps into a hole. Jo waves after her. Po holds his belly and laughs.*

## ACT I. Scene 3. *Huh?*

*Jo kicks Po three times in the gut, grabs his head.*

**JO**
*(Menacingly)*
You bag o' slop
Punch punch punch.

*Jo kisses Po's nose.*

Den kiss his wet nostril with a milk hoot
Ha ha ha and we both laugh.

*Low hum. PoJo stand like adults to address the Clouds.*

**JO**
The only thing I could detect was the silence.

**PO**
She was covered in blood.

**JO**
He had a shotgun blast to the back of his head.

**PO**
*(Innocent)*
Sprung from the loins of the wild ram and the netted bull, snakes are innocent children.

*Freebird rises with Foul Bird.*

**JO**
*(Wild, dancing)*
Carp, crocodile, shit of the sea. No one knows why we done it. Not even we.

**FREEBIRD**
*(Dour, accusatory, babyish)*
Matter Mutter matter shit
Shit wid the infant
Shit wid the babe
Shit in da booty
Shit in da grave
Matter Mutter matter shit

*(Pointing to Clouds)*
Power, power, power!

*Freebird exits. PoJo pull up their dicks and kiss their heads three times, giggle. Phone rings. PoJo don't understand the sound. Jo figures it out. Po fixes his eyebrows, plumps his hair, runs to answer.*

**POJO**
You an' me, brudda I cud love no odda.

**PO**
Yes.

**HAIRY WOMAN**
*(Hoarse, deep, German)*
Hello.
I was covered in blood, sons, but it weren't mine.

*PoJo, horrified, pitch phone into hole. Rings again. Silence. Ring. PoJo run screaming. On fifth ring, Harry rises. Low tone of wind.*

**HARRY**
*(Smug, confident, threatening)*
Payday, soldiers?

*(Clucks teeth)*
Not yet? Blind, emptying your load into shades, I see. Now, me, I prefers my own company. I likes the taste of me own body, me own blood and piss fouling the great unknown, eh?

*Harry sighs, squats, grunts. Picks up a boulder, grits teeth, moves it from one place to another. Each time he drops it, PoJo bounce.*

**JO**
*(Scruffy, irritated)*
What's you doing movin' those rocks?

**HARRY**
*(Pissed, accusatory)*
A day's labor.

**PO**
Well, quit.

**HARRY**
*(Smug, judgy)*
Some'm against work?

**JO**
Something against you, Tomato Face, fix yer eyes down. We ain't done nuttin'.

**HARRY**
Gotta get the job done.

*(Looking at Po, then Jo, then Clouds)*
Right!

*Sound of three blood drips. Low rumbling. Weeds rise, shaking.*

**HAIRY WOMAN**
What's he saying about me, boys?

**POJO**
Aaaaah!!!!!
Come again?

**HAIRY WOMAN**
So hungry down here.

*PoJo are running, huddling, circling, flapping arms like broken wings.*

**POJO**
Go 'way bad voice.

**HAIRY WOMAN**
*(Full, sexy)*
I can't bare the world singing without me. I'm too full of sex and love, son.

**POJO**
We-we-we ain't here, Ma. We're in da stars.
Like we told ya!

**HAIRY WOMAN**
I want to fuck, because I feel good.

*(Spirit cries)*
You have to get rid of me.

**POJO**
W-w-w-whaddya w-w-w-w-want?

**HAIRY WOMAN**
Som'pem eat.

*PoJo search for something. Jo finds a gummy worm in his pants, throws it at the grated floor below rabble. A holler is heard. PoJo quake, hold each other.*

*(Vaguely Austrian/Hungarian, furious)*
Horse fuckers! I'm so tired. Why make me repeat it all? I want to get out! He's the one who wants to become a horse fucker, your Father! Do you know I had a man whose cock was so big he had to have a friend hold it up for him, but it was nothing, nothing, when he put it in! I was back in the stars! They took me by the hand; they telepathically bathed me. It's no good darling, no good. It's just so ordinary, the whole zing. You offer me nothing, nothing special, chitchat, time passing, tempted fingers, yours and mine, woman and man.

*Metal bar bangs floor grating. Freebird's Foul Bird pops up—hideous, taunting.*

Nothing special!

**FREEBIRD**
Som'pem eat. Som'pem eat.
*(Cackles scornfully)*

**POJO**
Why, you unclean boid! We knews it was you!

*Jo grabs Foul Bird. Freebird moans, sobs. Jo pins Foul Bird, socks head. Po goes to finish the job, but stops.*

**HARRY**
*(Irish)*
To quote a Father, "I boned that old haggis downstairs like Mary on the cross—"

And next ...

*Weeds rise, shaking.*

*(Smacking lips)*
"I'm coming for you."

*Thunder. Smoke. Sound of chimes.*

ACT I. Scene 4. *Fish on a Stick*

SLEDGEWEED
*(Urgent)*
Oh, gods, Clouds, puffs of smoke.

*PoJo scuttle over to drop Foul Bird into Harry's hands. He falls backwards into hole. PoJo raise hands, Fosse-style.*

As I awoke I did hear the groans of branches—

Night pictures of horny old men and their shudder-doves.

*Panting. Thunder. Chimes (soft, chattering). Smell of frankincense, cologne, and semen.*

Necromancers, magicians, retirees, those with whittled plans and little on the clock. What portends this fat face greasing itself for the sun, de old Croaker, the Wand that did deform my life? He comes.

*Poseidon rises from below—sanguine, in yellow speedo. Harry rises to slither up the stage.*

POSEIDON
Say fellas, how's it goin'?
Genki deska?
Ah. Ha. Ha. Ha. I hope so. Ah. Ha. Ha. Ha. Pour me something stiff
I've got to have my head on today.
A corpse I should be
Fit, firm, and waxy. Gray.

*Poseidon tugs his "package."*

Secrets all tucked in.

*All shift positions—stiff, angular. Po sticks hand out as if to offer a drink, drops it.*

Oh, no? No dwinkie winkie?

Well. Huh.
Mind if I sit here?

*Alarmed, Harry pounds foot. PoJo sit straight up.*

JO
*(Stammering)*
Ere you a ghost?

*Poseidon gathers Ban de Soleil from air. Oils legs.*

PO
Jauntily, he creams himself and no answer.

**POSEIDON**
Hope not.

**JO**
Ere-ere-ere you ... a fadder of some kind, den?

**PO**
And on he goes creamin'.

*PoJo widen their mouths, turn to each other, wink, widen mouths.*

**JO**
Where are da goils, Dad?
Sea chicks?
Honkers?

*Poseidon crosses to stand at stage's edge. He thinks, pulls a cracker from the air, sniffs it, eats ravenously, snorting.*

**PO**
He stands at a ledge.

He's eatin'.

*Poseidon burps, pounds chest, wipes moustache.*

**JO**
Tins o' fingers, bankrupt rolls, sogged puddings, short meats, mist crackers with dusts, with his wet tips he dabs and smacks one by one while we churn and gape.

**PO**
*(Eager)*
I have a pig now, Daddy.

*Po, on his back, raises arms to Jo, who jumps on him. They become a single, crab-like entity—bodies chugging like a machine, reaching out to Poseidon, yowling.*

**POSEIDON**
Will you allow me a quiet death, fellas?
No? Well. Ugh. Blech.

*(Looks at Sledgeweed)*
Double ugh.

*Sledgeweed whimpers.*

Here comes the Deuce, I said to myself
Shuddering, wrested from a webbed sleep.
Spunk clusters, two sets of crooked arms
Wheelin' as one throat
A blade, headed toward me.

*Po moans.*

Frick and Frack with a hand out
Right, Daddy, where's the gum?

*Po cries.*

The Spit speaks.
Wish you'd never been born?
Well, file your complaint Droopy Drawers
And get back in line.

*Poseidon waves a finger as a mirror rises from a hole.*

**JO**
Look what you done! He's cryin'!

*He inspects himself.*

**POSEIDON**
And hello, Pretty Rage, look at your hips.

*Harry inches away.*

Jutted, sharp, right to the point.

*Harry and Sledgeweed cower.*

*(Falsetto)*
"Ain't nobody cryin'."
Oh, many a man have I reduced to tears
Soldiers, good men too
Men with heads on their necks
Not easy to fool
Generals, poets, pharmacists
I've taken ... right down.
That Christian God
He wanted it all the time.
Oh Clouds, now don't pretend you don't know me
I remember those pissy hands.

*(Sniffs, kneels)*
Undo something, will ya?
Make me work.
Louts, switches,
Saints o' the lost war,
Vectors of fashionable disease
Well, you lost, crowd.
You lost.
We're still dead and dying.

*Poseidon twists torso. Ass to audience, he turns head to look back. Freezes.*

**JO**
My fadder tilts da cavern at his hips
Twist-necks da slope of his back
Likes what he sees, all right.

*Poseidon postures, turns attention to Harry.*

**PO**
But Dad weren't a real man, if y'understand.
He was a false tad, a dab on the windowpane
A fleck, a spare, lying, always lying.

*Poseidon pursues Harry, who scuttles away with PoJo. Sledgeweed hops into a hole. Upstage Poseidon chases PoJo. Harry sits, watching.*

**POSEIDON**
Men, men, men, men, and men.
Not just any would I take
But inspected, I say,
Digits, nose, nails, and toes.
Those are what come off a man in the boil

The sea eats at pride
You, old son and stump, friend,
Are, how shall I say it? Bloated.
Too much meat in the sauce
A real man is as slender as the trace between sighs
High bellied, voiceless,
That is a man
Let him be ghost-like, air,
Let him skate past, an Image,
Only his Ideal counts

*(Arms raised, eyes roving)*
I could lose a quarter inch from my waist. Everyone says that behind my back. I know it. But they can't argue with these thighs, can they? Nope.

*PoJo gape.*

And now what is your wish, sons,
To pelt me with your sorrows?
Affect me with your upturned brows?

Oh. Ma. I know she's down there where I've kept her. The Night Mare, The Dank Hairs. The Dunkle Dame. Eyes and teeth, ALL woman. She round?

*Poseidon poses decoratively, freezes.*

**PO**
Judges, what you must think.

**JO**
*(Proper, as if in court, cleaned up, nervous)*
Your honor, I'm not sure the man was real.
I think he was a shade. You know what I mean? Honestly, your honor. He asked for blood. That's that that's what he asked for, ba-blood. I-I-believe that's c-c-ustomary.

*Po lies down beneath frozen Poseidon's spread legs.*

**PO**
*(Adult)*
I remember his legs above me, parted, the light playing on the silver hairs of his calves. Somebody in the kitchen laughed. "He's like a god," they said. "Like a Greek god." I don't think I can wait, I said. He said:

**POSEIDON**
Cool, let's wait.

*Poseidon and Jo cautiously exit, watching each other, whistling.*

**PO**
I peed in that hole and look, my semens come up bones.

*Po goes to the hole where Poseidon exited, sticks penis in—relief. He descends into the hole.*

*Harry pops up.*

**HARRY**
*(Frustrated, angry)*
Keep your seed outta da water, huh?
Gove'na? Right, y'honor?

*Sledgeweed's hands fan the edge of an upstage hole. She pulls herself up ("aaah"). PoJo rise from big hot tub. Freebird rises from downstage hole as a woman in a '30s-style bathing suit, jaded. Finally, Poseidon arises, holds court.*

**ACT II.** *Judges*
**Scene 1.** *Open-toed show*

**POSEIDON**
Your mother—

*All sigh, moan.*

You heard how she went to court against herself, and lost, naturally. In that fur, that white-eyed fox, that stole, bosoms heaving, she quakes "Yoo-hoo! Your honor, your honor! Yoo-hoo! Your honor!" She waddles to the bench, kneels, "The old woman was so loud, your honor, so loud. I hate the old woman downstairs. She's always coughin'."

*Freebird drops into hole.*

You hear her from a mile away.

*(Imitates cough)*
I sez there's a war on. Maybe soldiers would like to get some sleep. Ugh. "She's a dog." She talks in the loudest voice like this: "A mother's blood was spilt! Will there be no vengeance?!" Like she's on TV, for God sakes. I mean for goodness sakes, pardon me, Judges. She reads like this:

**SLEDGEWEED**
Cat bat rat fat.

**POSEIDON**
What's she—she's learnin' to read?—oh, that big dummy. We don't need to know these animals.

**SLEDGEWEED**
*(Mocking, covering growing fear)*
You know who's stickin' her, but good? You know who's doin' her laundry? Her own—

*All gasp.*

Your honor, I won't dignify yer court wit dese macerations, but she's doin' it to her own—

*All gasp.*

**POSEIDON**
No, not correct. She is chaste, solemn. Severe.

*Harry crawls out of hot tub hole. Freebird pops up from another hole with a drink and a joint.*

**HARRY**
And she's huge! She's enormous. She's a whale. She's a crusher. They're gonna have to get her outta that basement with a crane. Where are the cameras?

*(Coyly)*
I guess that would be my question, your honor. Is this on tape?

*Harry laughs loudly. Poseidon glares. All hush.*

**SLEDGEWEED**
*(To Poseidon)*
But that's you. Isn't it?

**POSEIDON/HAIRY WOMAN**
No, it isn't. I had children. I suffered.

**FREEBIRD**
*(Drinking)*
Sing it, brother.

**SLEDGEWEED**
*(Sliding toward Clouds)*
Uh, I'm double-parked, your honor. Couldeth I go?

**POSEIDON**
No!

**HARRY**
He's not finished.

**POSEIDON**

And you, Harry. Soldier, corporal. You, you ... you ... rank. Remember?

**SLEDGEWEED**

I don't believe in love, Daddy.

**POSEIDON**

I believe in it. I'm desperate for it! She. She had something ...

*(Containing himself, looking at PoJo)*

Your mother was a dolt, a grade-A blot. "Your honor"— Get this, judges!—"Your honor," she yip-yaps, panting, with that condition o' hers. "Down there in the basement, every'ting is me, de old washin' board, de cock-a-roach, da ball of fuzz, da liquor bottles, da cracks in the sea-ment, da boxing gloves—what am I supposed to do? Live like this? I'm full of life, your honor! I'm a woman!"

*Poseidon turns, freezes.*

**SLEDGEWEED**

Clouds, why wasn't I allowed to pull da twigger! Why wasn't I allowed to avenge her, when I coulda done it good!

*Poseidon howls, waves hands, poses, makes others howl.*

**ALL**

We're all wolves, your honor! Wolves!!

**FREEBIRD**

*(Annoyed)*

I'm not howling.

*Poseidon exits. PoJo go into separate holes; their heads appear above, in profile. Exit Freebird. Harry pounds on stage, glaring at Sledgeweed, who isn't sure why. Exit Harry. Pulsing begins at far end of stage. Sledgeweed runs toward it.*

**SLEDGEWEED**

Ma, you up and run. Or did dey d'own you? I listens, but you get me no speech. Ma. You great big hairy brute! Dey done milked you, and now youse got me in dis getup, clickin' off time. You da demon shitting in da bed! You da devil with da drippin' fangs! You da master of da unrulies, but you laying low, snake! Hrumph! Youse betters haul outta dat cave when dey come to 'tack. Oh, dey feels me Ma, and dats why dey's mash me. Poor wil' crush-station all alone on dis moiderous plank. Ma! You come. He's possess you, Ma, and when he does, he's owns us all.

*Freebird rises, holding candy mic. Poseidon rises—delicate, older. Sledgeweed runs away.*

**FREEBIRD**
How'd ya feel about da judgment, huh? What a skirt steak. Lady, you got spanked. Think you'll do real time?

*Freebird, cynically heart-broken, exits. Poseidon tries to open trapdoor. Jo trundles over to him.*

**POSEIDON**
No pictures, please. It's over.

**JO**
Ma, lemme, lemme, help you.

**POSEIDON**
I'm fine, dear.

**JO**
Just lemme—

**POSEIDON**
I told you—!

*Poseidon throws Jo against the wall with superhuman strength. He then opens a pair of trapdoors to reveal a fur-lined interior. Po awakens and gasps—fascinated. He minces downstage, takes Poseidon's arm, lowers him into interior.*

I'm fine.

**PO**
Mother, may I take your arm?

**POSEIDON/HAIRY WOMAN**
Oh, sank you darling. My ankle. Oh.

**ACT II. Scene 2.** *He vas vonderful!*

*Flute (romantic passage, then dark fairy-tale). Hairy Woman rises in unfastened yellow bikini top. Po goes to tie the back, excited.*

**PO**
Mutter, Matter, Mudder, sitting there in the back room with a handful of photos, blonde as the devil.

**HAIRY WOMAN**
Zat krazy Kissinger. I slept with him.

**PO**
Is that right?

**HAIRY WOMAN**
He vas vonderful.

**PO**
I knew she was lying.

**HAIRY WOMAN**
*(Luringly)*
Sit close to me.

**PO**
Mudder, you know I have to keep my powers.

**HAIRY WOMAN**
Of course.

*Po and Hairy Woman exchange words in private.*

**PO**
Mutti—
Our secret language!

*Jo sleeps. Freebird rises, speaks wistfully in German, wags her tongue at Jo, exits.*

**HAIRY WOMAN**
What beauties! My horses! You know nothing but to sit on them and step wonderfully! Mr. Nixon wanted my white horse, but I said, Mr. Nixon, you have everything, can you really take my white horse too?

**PO**
*(Merrily)*
You had him there.

*Po dips out of sight, then gradually reemerges, his hands reaching toward Hairy Woman's breasts.*

**HAIRY WOMAN**
I did. Oh, can you imagine. So many men, darling, only want company, even your father.

**PO**
Oh, Mudda. Why did we have to come to dis doity place?

**HAIRY WOMAN**
Everywhere dere are mirrors, darling, black walls. Dose backroom smokies are doing dere

unspeakables. Dey'll murder us in our sleep, son. We must keep togeder, you and I, and da beer, dear, please. Get me one.

**PO**
Mudder, you are so small. You are as long as my finga. You're like dose little gnomes dat come out at night and sit on your glasses frames. May I captcha you?

**POSEIDON/HAIRY WOMAN**
Son, I'm not real.

*Po hurls himself into childish tantrum.*

**PO**
Oh, darn it. I wanted a glasses gnome!

**HAIRY WOMAN**
Son, poor, son, you have no idea what I suffered coming to this unforgiving country hiding in a barrel. If I died, my parents would feel. I couldn't do that to them. They were beautiful people who deserved to forget, and that's my story, son.

*Sustained D-note as Hairy Woman lowers herself into trapdoor, holding breath. Blade of Grass grows. Jo reaches out to Po. Holding hands, they roll upstage, grunting and groaning, until Po falls into a hole. Jo stretches out beside it. Sledgeweed rises, sees long Blade.*

**ACT II. Scene 3.** *Mist and rain*

**SLEDGEWEED**
*(Scared at possibility of happiness and reunion)*
Is that you? Is that you, Ma?

*Rain.*

**ACT III.** *HARD*
**Scene 1.** *I tried, I tried, Lord knows I tried …*

*Hairy Woman emerges from the fur-lined interior, gasping, crying hard.*

**JO**
You want me to take the garbage out?

**HAIRY WOMAN**
*(Suddenly recovering)*
Your father's crying again.

He and I, we barely kissed. After you were born. He's not even funny. Do you laugh at his jokes? I don't.

*(Laughs)*
How long will you be ... doing what you do?

**JO**
*(Mature)*
Six months, a year. Dunno. I don't know!

**HAIRY WOMAN**
You were so big, darling. You torn my ass.

**JO**
*(Affectless)*
Heard it. I'm innocent. I didn't do anything!

**HAIRY WOMAN**
Now I can't hold my pee. Do you know dat?

**POSEIDON**
A man fucks me, and I pee.

**HAIRY WOMAN**
Now I made a joke. Tanks for dat. For da funny.

**JO**
*(Hopeful)*
You were my first. Crazy. Crazy son of a bitch to kill me on my own sofa. What did I do? Because I'm strong? A fighter? Because you never missed a meal? Sometimes, I think I should strike back.

*Hairy Woman moves toward Jo, who goes onto his back like a baby seeking an embrace. She holds him by the shoulders. Jo giggles a little hysterically, somewhere between a baby getting love and an adult being rejected. Laughing, Hairy Woman closes the trapdoors one at a time.*

**HAIRY WOMAN**
I think I can't do anything but haunt you. Yes. You'll be walking down da street, chewing that awful gum, like a big lump in your cheek, and you will see me, at the corner of your eye in a bakery window, like when I was a girl, young, innocent. You will think, oh my god, that stupid girl looks just like my mother, I should go and kill her too, and then ... I laugh thinking about the disaster that will come upon you. On your head. Your children will be born so stupid. Dey won't even know how to flush a toilet. My god. Cretins. Dey will look out at the world and gape and stare like monsters. Like dis. Duh. Duh. Duh.
*(Laughs)*

**POSEIDON**
*(Becoming male, a father, with backhand slap on head)*
Hey, numbskull—

**ACT III. Scene 2.** *My ting's achin'*

*Jo wakes up—startled like a baby—stands, stomps. Po enters stomping. They look at each other, and splat!—like lizards—attach themselves to opposite walls. Jo lights a joint.*

**OLD SPLINTERS**
Ow! Ow! Ow!

**JO**
You want some?

**PO**
Naw.

**JO**
Brudda?

He put his hairy palm on my chest. I waited.
I waited, but nothing happened.

*Jo strides across the stage, hits Po's stomach, pinches his nose, blows smoke. Po chokes, slides down the wall. Jo lays down, smokes. Po stews—he wants him. Jo considers it, rises, and leans against the wall with arms over Po's head. Lovingly, he strokes Po's dick with his foot, then gradually steps on it harder and harder. Po screams. Jo crushes Po's head between his thighs. Po yells. Jo walks away. Po grabs his ankle, trips him. Jo tries to fight back, but Po punches his head, pins him down, threatens him with his dick.*

**PO**
Who won?!
Brudda. My ting's achin'.

**JO**
So?

**PO**
Suck it.

*Freebird pops up.*

**FREEBIRD**
*(Cynically)*
Say, Pieface, there's a delicate hand on yer knob. Why not turn it?

*Jo stomps away. Po mirrors him—frustrated, charged.*

**JO**
*(Confronting Clouds)*
Judges. Stop me if I told you this—

*Low-frequency sound. Jo begins to disassociate and wobble.*

*Poseidon and Sledgeweed rise. He holds two white fans, she holds two sprigs of seaweed. Flute starts (like squeaky wheels).*

**POSEIDON**
Let's start with the boudoir.

Out of the thick Breath, out of ...
Swirling desire ...

**FREEBIRD**
*(Scratchy '30s radio, or muted Taylor Swift)*
Mutter is bees crawin'. Mudder is heart pappin'.

*Po is in a hole. Jo gets in behind, fucks him. Jo bobs head as Po cups his ears.*

**PO**
I let my brother fuck me in the bathtub.

Even da mailman retreat when he saw dat letter comin' out of my house. Letter widout a body. When he saw da Woid movin' fast—

He sitting dere in IV housing
Wid a headset on.
Daddy? Daddy, I said ... he weren't be in IV housing if he weren't dis way. Lil spot of da devil in 'em, don't you t'ink?

*Poseidon and Sledgeweed get out of hole and squat.*

**JO**
Dad said:

**POSEIDON**
Put in it, man. We don't got all day.

*Po uses Jo's lizard tail as a guitar.*

**JO**
*(Singing)*
Den one night on a scryin' wall I saw dem in Daddy's eyes
Da roll call o' tears:

**POSEIDON**
*(Singing, Kentucky porch-style)*
And now they're comin' for me. Sons, I forgot to tell ya, I done it. *I forgot to tell ya, sons.*

**PO**
*(Sung and spoken)*
Matthew, Luke, Mark, David, and John. Jorge, Benji, Scott, Elliot, Leonard, Dirk, Rick, Sean, and on and on and on. Daniel, Martin, Mario, Evan, Gale, Gary, Pete, Jack. Names.

*(Dumb, awed)*
How do men have such names?

*Po pounds out a beat. Jo moves snake-like on his belly.*

**JO**
*(Singing diabolically)*
Night dey creep back, hungry shades, all smiles. Gimme gimme gimme.

**ALL MEN**
*(Barbershop quartet-style)*
Whassup? Whassup? Whassup? Whassup? Whaaaaa—ssup?

**SLEDGEWEED**
*(Rough, whispered)*
Hey, don't drink da water!

**POSEIDON**
*(Scratchy)*
Never did pay dem bills.

**PO**
*(Singing)*
Gotta pay the piper, Pop.

**JO**
*(Singing)*
And a veil of salt water thread the sky.
Oh. Daddy's crying again.

**POJO**
*(Singing—sad, protracted)*
Oh, Daddy. Oh, Dad.

**POSEIDON**
*(Scratchy)*
Never did pay dem bills.

*(In afterthought)*
Hey, numbskull, I done it.

I kilt her, son.
Can you just forget it, huh?
Can you just get on with your life?

*Exit Poseidon.*

**JO**
*(Scared, uncomprehending, thumb in mouth)*
I need you to take that thumb out of your mouth, soldier.

**PO**
*(Scared, uncomprehending, thumb in mouth)*
Come again?

**JO**
I need you to remove that goddamn thumb.

**PO**
*(Mocking)*
I need you to remove that goddamn thumb, soldier.

**JO**
Hey. Hey.

*Po ignores Jo, who stretches his arm out like a gun.*

*(More urgently, poignantly)*
Hey.

Bang.

*Po slumps in his hole.*

**ACT III. Scene 3.** *Not long for dis woild*

*Strong smell of the ocean. Sound of rain. Sledgeweed rises with silken tube pulled over her head, searching and consuming food. Styrofoam Cup comes up bobbing, followed by Fleeting Beings. Heads of the Four Shades appear in the stage's far distance.*

**SHADES**
*(All together, seductive)*
Hey, babe. Whassup?

You look fabulous.

*Po awakens, inspired.*

Goin' to the liquor store?
What about me?
Let's make it three.
Can I come too?

**PO**
*(Looking into hole)*
Brudda, I know that's you hidin' there.

**SHADES**
*(Vampire-like)*
Aw, kid, we won't hurt you.
Just foolin' around. We're not real.
Shades is all.
Just want a drop, babe, a dab, you knows.
Get through the night.
It's lonesome out here.

**PO**
Brother, no, it's not today
We are no longer One Thing, no, we will be Two.

**SHADE**
*(Like Poseidon)*
Ah, faggot.

*Po curls up.*

Fuck off, bitch
Bor-*ring*.
Suck me.
Die.

*Po slowly rolls to his "death."*

**ACT III. Scene 4.** *Stiffed*

*Freebird and Harry rise.*

**FREEBIRD**
Over to Winchell's I knews a guy
Wid a lip hanging like so, slice of tomato danglin'.
Everybody know, Harry Oh, Harry Who Tomato Face.

**HARRY**
*(Singing)*
Two boys, two boys, two boys went down to sea
The sea, the sea, the deadly ponderous sea
Last seen inside the sea

Last seen inside the sea
The boys lacked confidence
The boys lacked careful speech
Rarely seen or heard
They shot into the breach

*Sledgeweed watches lustfully as Harry reaches for Po's dick. He stops himself.*

*(Horrified)*
My hands get stiff,
Slug, stiff in the jernts.
Should be your job, Snifter, to take the curs'ed to their beds. No, it's Harry Who Tomato Face must labor on.

*(For Po's benefit, priestly, Irish)*
Poor fossils, all hushed now, gods lil chirren, usta dream 'bout sticking Ma and Pa in the kettle. Now look, grass grows over their sacred hearts, leathery entrails, positioned in such a way as to foretell a dubious end for two twins, scaly friends, who love each other a little too much, if you see as I do.

*Sledgeweed climbs Harry's leg, feels him.*

**SLEDGEWEED**
Seems to me it's your hammer doin' da bonkin', Thug. Seems to me you mighta clobbered Ma and Pa for money, or is it *love?*

**HARRY**
*(Repulsed, dropping pretense)*
Oh, daddies are always dying. I'd take him to Hell twice, if he paid me. The devil loves a wrinkled bosom.

*(Obscenely)*
It's the crush what makes us sick, Slug—and sicker.

*Harry—stiff, tense—rejects her. Sledgeweed gathers herself, exits solemnly.*

**SLEDGEWEED**
Don't nobody love you wit dat great big prick o' yours? Nobody gobbled you up yet?

**ACT III. Scene 5.** *Homegrown*

*Harry is moving imaginary boulders from one place to another, with much effort.*

**JO**
*(Relieved adult)*
Ah. Awesome.
Gotta smoke?

**HARRY**
Smokes? That's for the tony set, son, not for Ol' One Shoe.

**JO**
Can I help with the rocks?

**HARRY**
*(Laughing)*
I wouldn't touch those.

**JO**
Zat how you got hooked?

**HARRY**
*(Nodding)*
Tryin' to do my part.

*Harry suspiciously watches Po.*

**JO**
Say, did you used to be somebody? I mean, before?

**HARRY**
Not really.
Sold automobiles.

**JO**
One or two I bet?

**HARRY**
Muybe.

*Silence.*

**JO**
Aren't you gonna ask about me?

**HARRY**
Let's see.

Married, love your wife. Have a kid, 'bout three. Like having your kicks on the DL once in a while. Grindr, Blendr, Tinder, don'matter. Love a carne asada burrito, da works, Coke, Diet Coke now 'at yer in yer forties. Can't do as many push-ups, but still wiry. You got powers, like running at incredible speeds, imitating a dog, red belt in Judo, Jujitsu, Karate, Kung Fu, Krav Maga. Used to be a wedding photographer, played in a band, covers mostly, but still a helluva lotta fun. How'd I do?

**JO**
*(Embarrassed)*
Shit, man, that was totally wrong.

**HARRY**
Well, just a stab.

*(Referring to Po's body, dead at the lip of the stage)*
Now, him. What's his game?

**JO**
Some dude.

**HARRY**
Wouldn't be so sure. He's up to somethin'.

**JO**
I guess.

**HARRY**
*(Eyes to Clouds)*
And them on the hill. You can be sure whatever it is they're up to, plans don't include you.
You need love, son?

**JO**
Yeah.

**HARRY**
Someone who sees you.

**JO**
Yeah.

**HARRY**
But who'd do that? Who'd take the time?

**JO**
I dunno.

**HARRY**
You've been pegged.

**JO**
Yeah.

**HARRY**
You're not like they say.

**JO**
I know.

**HARRY**
It's just hard is all.

**JO**
Yeah.

**HARRY**
Hard life, moving forward, invisible, checking for quarters in pay phones, dimes in the cracks of sidewalks, that's the dream, finding a big one, a C-note caught on a rosebush in the park. It could happen, though. I've heard tell.

*Poseidon rises from big hole, winks at Harry.*

**JO**
Yeah.
*(Begins weeping)*

*Harry strokes Jo's head as he falls asleep in his lap. As soon as Jo is unconscious, Harry wipes his hands, disgusted. Sound of moving water. Po awakens, starts crawling. Harry does too. They eye each other. Poseidon appears in big hole as a woman bathing. Sledgeweed appears in a nearby hole, also as a woman. They're tired of each other. PoJo fall asleep together. Harry sits confidently.*

**HARRY**
If you was my son …

## ACT III. Scene 6. *Desperados*

*Sledgeweed and Hairy Woman sit with their feet dangling in holes.*

**SLEDGEWEED**
I told you we shouldn't have come back.
Saltine?

**HAIRY WOMAN**
No. I'm sick. I told you. I'm sick.

**SLEDGEWEED**
Well, that's why I offered it.

**HARRY**
"The little fly cleans his legs, back and fore
In the growing shadow, playfully,
Unaware of the Titan's coming."
Who said that?

**SLEDGEWEED**
You, I guess. Your sons—

**HAIRY WOMAN**
Anomalies. Shoulda pitched them in the drink.

**SLEDGEWEED**
Look at that sky. Empty.

*Sledgeweed dips a finger in water below. Sound of a ripple.*

I let my hand wander
Everything's tight, afraid.
Like sticking my hand in water,
Hiding that flickering tail,
My finger, flashing like a scimitar, then—

*Sledgeweed pulls up a piece of Jo's tail.*

**HAIRY WOMAN/POSEIDON**
*(Vitriolic)*
Dose are my boys, my sons.

**SLEDGEWEED**
You'll have more.

*Harry rises.*

**HARRY**
I'm taking one.

*Poseidon laughs. Harry moves in on Sledgeweed seductively.*

**HAIRY WOMAN**
Not da little one.

**SLEDGEWEED**
Hey, don't ... you ain't her.

*Reluctantly, Sledgeweed gives him a piece of Jo's tail.*

**HARRY**
Thanks.

*Freebird rises, in baby diapers.*

**FREEBIRD**
Twee, twee, twee
I'm a lil bab-ee
When I tawk like dis
e'wee ting so much betta
Yeah, well, fuck you den
Gimme M&M

How 'bout a piece o' plastic?
Cunts.

**SLEDGEWEED**
Oh, Devil, dat's not you.

**FREEBIRD**
I know.

**SLEDGEWEED**
You was a nice boid.

*Exit Freebird followed by Sledgeweed.*

**FREEBIRD**
I know.

## ACT III. Scene 7. *Oh, that's why*

*Po awakens—human—looks at Jo, touches him, exits without looking back. Jo remains sleeping between two holes, from which Poseidon and Harry rise—gods in his dream. They entice each other, handling, licking, and biting Jo.*

**POSEIDON**
Men like you can't even
Walk down their own streets.
Just tryin' to gather a moment is all—

**HARRY**
Would you be interested?

**POSEIDON**
Would you like to swing a bat?
I see your energies have been diminished—

**HARRY**
Eating all that chicken, that pork ... that dog?

**POSEIDON**
Would you be interested in seeing the date
of your death?

**HARRY**
But if you knew like I know—

**POSEIDON**
What I'm trying to do—

**HARRY**
What he's trying to do—

**POSEIDON**
What I'm tryin' to do is get you to see—

**HARRY**
There're two types of men—

**POSEIDON**
Them that do's and them that's done in.
Which are you, buster?
Why back in the day—

**HARRY**
Back in the day—

**POSEIDON**
You can see from our scars—there are opposing teams.

**HARRY**
Did you lose that memory?
Are you playin' a game?

**POSEIDON**
Did you say everything's cool,
I'll be home for Christmas?
Well, what's under that tree, fella?

**HARRY**
Still betting on that primal wound
To get your stock up?
Yogurt? Donut? Breathatarian?

**POSEIDON**
Don't know what's good for you?
Well, you'll drink nothing but fresh water if you do
And stay away from that shore.

**HARRY**
Let the Clouds buoy you
Seek their applause
They know morality from decay.

**POSEIDON**
Tell me the truth, tell me—

HARRY
You like to see a white man swing?
Dontcha? Dontcha?

POSEIDON
Why do you think I glow in the dark?
So's you can pick me out, son.

HARRY
And here's another thing.

POSEIDON
You ain't getting paid,
Right?

POSEIDON
Listen to your old dad.

HARRY
And your Gran'pappy too.

POSEIDON
That's right. He knew.

HARRY
Fought in every war, just like you.

POSEIDON
And you're still marching in place!

HARRY
How 'bout some singing with that praise? Eh?

POSEIDON
Soldier?

HARRY
Be nice to the boogeyman.

POSEIDON
You never know what he can do for ya!

*Exit Poseidon and Harry. Po's head rises from hole—vacant, expressionless. Freebird appears and pleasures him.*

## Act IV. *High Everybody*
## Scene 1. *Raw and ready*

*Jo sits up, awake. Lights become ordinary.*

**JO**

Hi everybody. It's nice to be here tonight. So, uh, wow, it's so cool to just ... ha ... ah ... wow.

No matter what you've done in your life, you're forgiven, right? I mean, that's the way I look at it. Wow, like I'm not sure if I wanna sing, or ... haha. Geez, Clouds. Yeah. No matter what you've done—you're just a baby, right? Just innocent. That lil smile. Maybe it's gas. But I don't believe that. I believe we're all just doing our best, and we can be forgiven. Have I used up my time? Brother, why don't you come out here?

**PO**

*(Interrupting, affectless)*

This is what I said: Make me stupid. That's what I asked, specifically: Please make me stupid. Remember. Talk, argue, do whatever, just leave me out of it. I want no thoughts, no ideas, no nothing, not even feelings, except pleasure. I want everybody, one by one, to pleasure me. Play with my butthole, feed me, get me things I want ... and that's it.

*During the following, Po will smoke and get a tail stroke, a head massage, and be fed grapes.*

**JO**

Well, okay then. Dis guy. Wow. Let's have a hand. Shoot, you know. Yes, yes, yes, I think I killed my—birth people. But I killed so fucking many people it's like crazy, right? I mean, you've done that, so ... cool. Yeah, it's ... I'm not a bad person. That's the first thing. I'm not. Just like you are not, your honors. So, you can't say that. Only I know that. And you and I, both being killers and whatnot, we're still very different. Because for me it was more like—damn, I wish you would just get up here, bro, and back me up, dude.

*Po barks or does nothing or smiles.*

*(Attempting to contain rage)*

Okay, so he's off the list.

Right now. Like, he's done. Everybody down with that? You saw that, right?

He's a fucking prick. Because he will leave you out to hang. I said, where's that thumb, soldier? He did not show it to me, your honors, as I requested. I was in the zone. His eyes.

I love that fucker. I love him. You do not understand this. He and I fucking fell down here from the same star or whatnot. Like who knows. We don't know where the fuck we're from. How the hell do you expect me to give a goddam exception speech, your honor, if I do not know the crime I am herewith being fucking charged with. I am okay to be in the movie, just let me have the damn script!

*Po barks a little. Stops.*

Your honor. Well, these shades, see. They requested me to proceed to bring them blood. If you've followed my career, you know that is how I roll. That's what I do.

*(Singing)*
"You know darn well I was a snake before you let me in."

I've taken your time, and you can never get it back. I get that. Just one more thing. You have failed me, Clouds, in every respect. I was in the sky slicing, kicking, choking, thrusting, banging, breathing hard, our pride, our bane, you said. Well, I died and died again, but there was no celebration, no wail, no sadness except from one, who secreted her tears beneath the earth in black pools of glossy lacrimon or whatthefuck that I'm fucking supposed to say. Okay, boss men, fornicators, lovers of a partial god, I hold you, Clouds, guilty of whisking yourselves away just in time. Shall I speak? Shall I say more? Shut up you say? You already read about me? Well done. No more. Zip. I retreat.

*Jo stomps on trapdoor. It opens, he exits, dropping his water bottle, which rolls toward Rabble. Po exits.*

**Act IV. Scene 2.** *I got you babe*

*Freebird scoots out of a trapdoor, takes off wig to become Chelsea. Sledgeweed rises. Chelsea helps her take off her breast rig. Sledgeweed becomes Zut.*

**ZUT**
Whew. I'm glad that's over. I was a little scared at first but then I got into it.

CHELSEA
*(Nuzzling Zut)*
Why were you scared, though?

ZUT
*(Scooting closer)*
I don't know, I thought maybe ... I don't know. Maybe I could catch some feelings or something, like get caught up.

CHELSEA
*(Scooting away)*
Well, you know, I just try to remember it's a play.

ZUT
Right. Right, right. If I were free to say what I really want, I'd—

CHELSEA
But you can't do that.

ZUT
Right. Why not?

CHELSEA
Because I'd stop it. I'd police you.

ZUT
Let's not confuse entertainment with moral instruction.

CHELSEA
Let's not give ourselves over to work that makes no demands.

ZUT
What were you saying, sorry?

CHELSEA
Is that your finger?

ZUT
What?

CHELSEA
I thought ... that's not your finger?

**ZUT**
*(Confused)*
No.

**CHELSEA**
That *is* your finger.

*Chelsea and Zut wave their hands while Peaseashit and Styrofoam Cup push them up by the ass.*

**ZUT**
No. My finger is here. Look! This is my finger.

**CHELSEA**
Then what's up my ass?

**PEASEASHIT AND STYROFOAM CUP**
*(Hysterical)*
Eden's saved!

*Drumming. Upbeat singing. Stage spouts water as Zut and Chelsea twerk over holes.*

**Act IV. Scene 3.** *Get your coats and parking stubs*

*Jo appears as Joe pulling up Golden Tube. At its other end is Poseidon—ancient, wobbly, theatrical, with two shriveled silver balls attached to his enormous phallus. Joe yanks him along while humming Soviet work song.*

**POSEIDON**
*(Shaky British)*
How lovely to find oneself engorged at world's end. Judges, I have but one defendant hanging on.

*(Coughing, stumbling)*
And how I would like to try him.

*Trapdoor to fur-lined interior whams open: It's Po in red wig and foppish yellow suit.*

Oh, you scared me! I thought you were a carb.

**PO**
Mater/Pater, you misconstrue. Tis I, the Lizard Man, scraped into a rockin' pantsuit, returned for a last laugh. I refused you, but the tide hurled me back. Come, Brudda, let me helfe you out of dis stinking ship. Sharp death seeks but whom? You? You?

*(Pointing)*
You?
Clouds, forgive my rudeness in offering up a simple man. If I offend, twas only for my own great delight—or so I'm told by tyrant page in black and white.

**JO**
*(Shakespearean)*
And may I too seek a reprieve? I've gorged on your confinement, and I repent.

*PoJo kiss.*

**SLEDGEWOOD**
*(Appearing and disappearing)*
So stoopid.

**PO**
Father, Mother has transformed us into a love act repulsive to you.

**POSEIDON**
She's made you soft, barely detectable.

**PO**
Au contraire. We've killed you in our dreams and now, alas, in the ... rotting flesh.

**POSEIDON**
*(Brooklyn)*
Ah, save it for the stage.

*Po hits Old Splinters emphatically three times.*

**PO**
Father, this *is* the stage.
Terror! That's the news.
Your vial.

**POSEIDON**
Well, you're disgusting.

**PO**
*(Producing vial velcroed to glove)*
Accept your vial, Father.

**POSEIDON**
Ah. I do. And here it is again, Pater's final hour. I've played the part often and to great effect. Here are the reviews.

*Freebird rises.*

**FREEBIRD**
*(Walter Winchell-style)*
"Nep's tune hasn't changed."
"Boards groan in croak scene."
"Actor found dead in paper bag."

*Dolphins rise, bob in holes.*

**POSEIDON**
*(Loud, fierce, sucking in air and releasing it—supernatural)*
Look at this body, eons old
Living on breath and breath alone
You've never seen a progenitor quite like me
Riding dolphins to infinity!

Let me ride those bubble butts to oblivion
Joy! Joy! Joy!

**Act IV. Scene 4.** *And now the end is*

*Dark blue light. Sound of oars. Harry appears rowing.*

**POSEIDON**
Do I know you? Did we—

**HARRY**
Probably.

**POSEIDON**
I'm sure you were excellent. Are we—

*Harry grunts in affirmative.*

Well, then row faster.

**HARRY**
No boat, friend.
See the sign: "For mental comfort only."

**POSEIDON**
Ah.

**HARRY**
Poseidon, leader of men,
Or so he thinks in his rocking tomb.

**POSEIDON**
*(Holds vial, drinks, feels effects of poison)*
Oh, great lover of life
Deadly poison, I drink of thee

Out of my great love
My great compassion
I take it on.

*Harry laughs at Poseidon's arrogance.*

Nothing as pure as the rape of a lemon, I say.
The perfect fruit.

*Poseidon puts his hand out for a lemon. It appears. He tries to peel the lemon, but it resists. He claps his hands, disappearing it.*

**HARRY**
I remember when we was young and drunk, comin' out of the bar, laughing. There he was, an old man at forty-two, marked with disease, and you gasped. Look at you now, warping your mouth the same way.

**POSEIDON**
Ah, guilt. Doesn't work. I'm pleased.
I don't have the guts to go into old age.
Look at you. You're so lucky. You're already ruined.

**HARRY**
You thought, "I'm a most remarkable piece of flotsam and jetsam." You turned out to be just about that.

**POSEIDON**
The beauty of sick
One strives for titanic impermeability
Christ, sword in hand, admits no front entry
Vigilant, he guards his privates!
And receives his blossoms at the back door
Puckered roses, skin dances,
Something smeared across tomorrow never comes
Oh, it comes all right. It comes.
I'm glass. I'm mirror. I'm rain.
I'm a god, fellas, and I'll be back again.

**HARRY**
Silence all filled up by squeals of pleasure, they rowed on.

*Fade to black.*

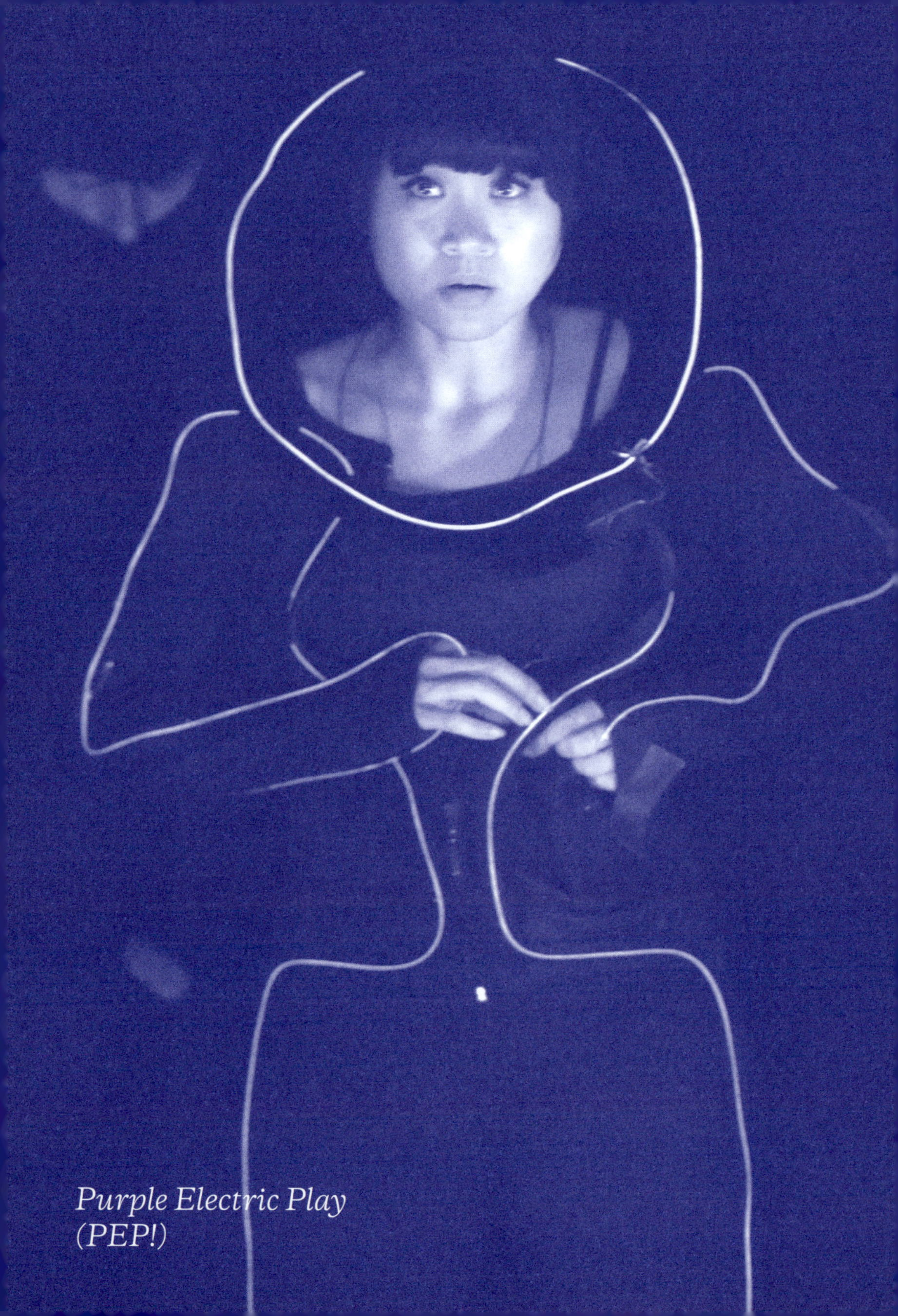

*Purple Electric Play (PEP!)*

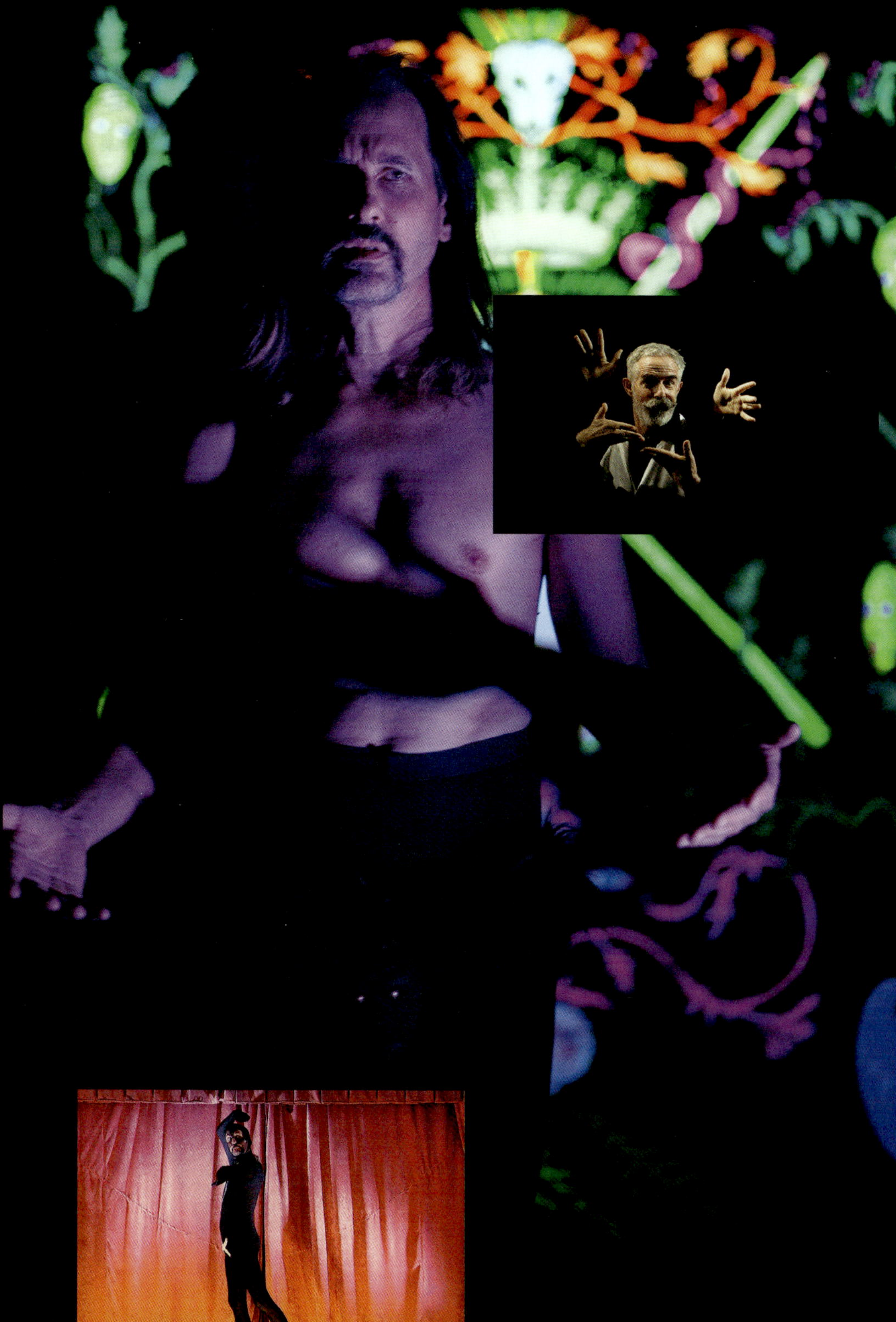

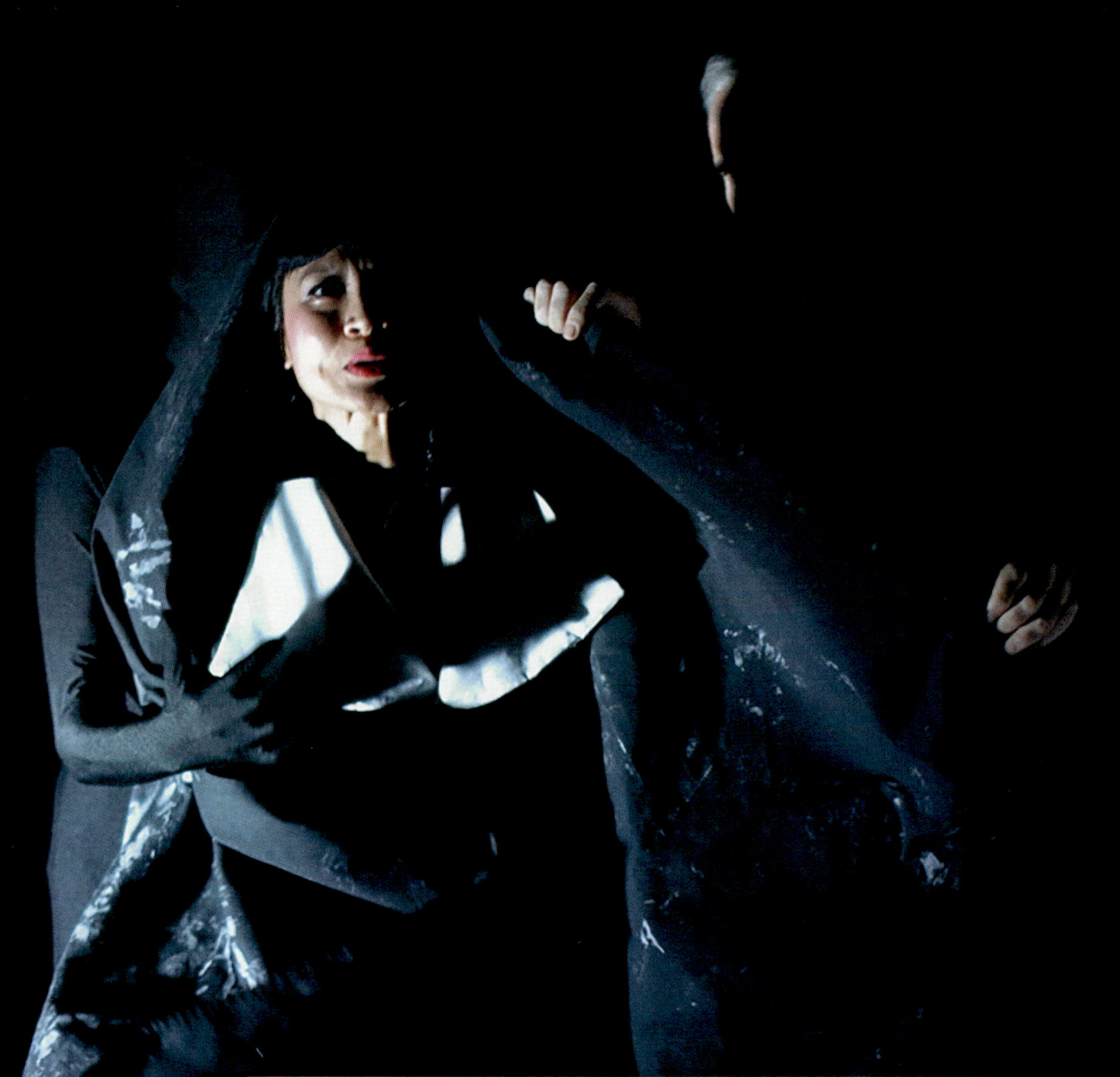

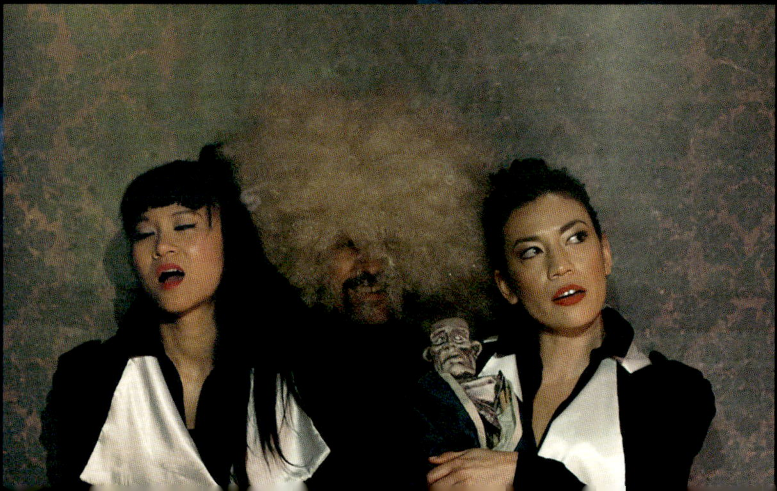

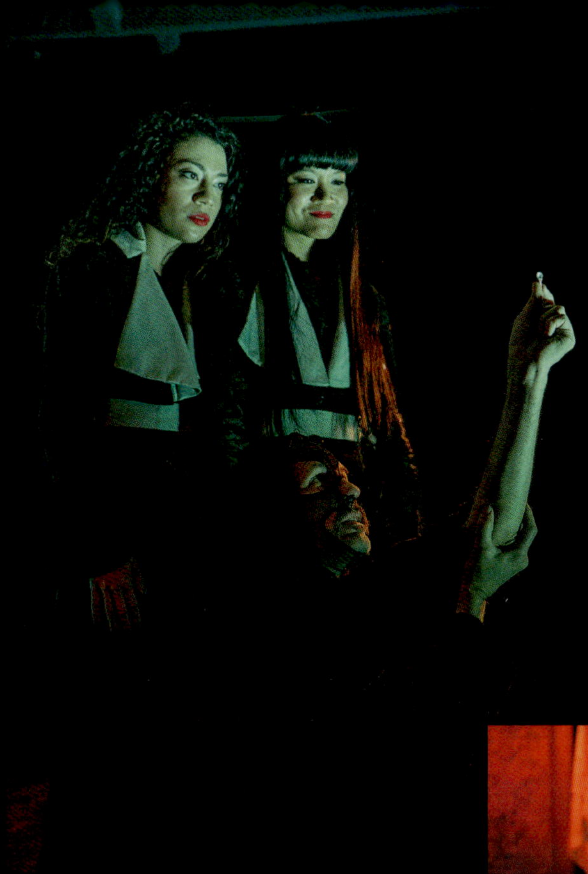

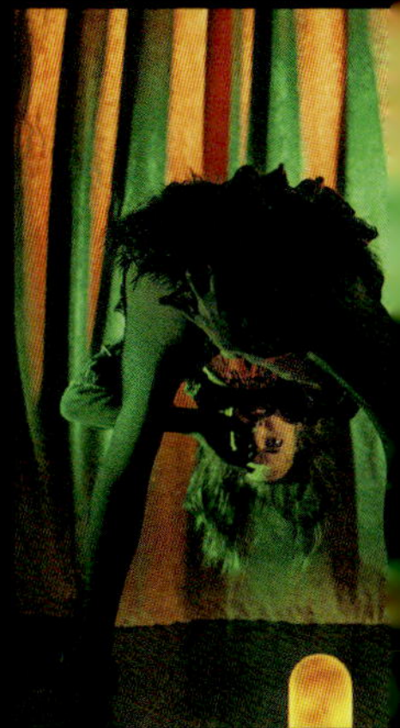

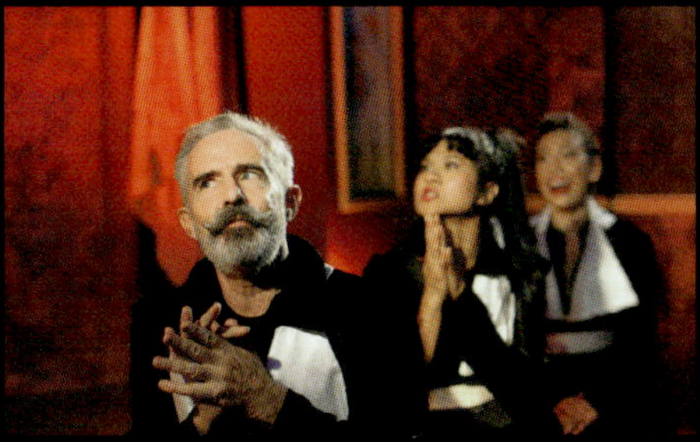

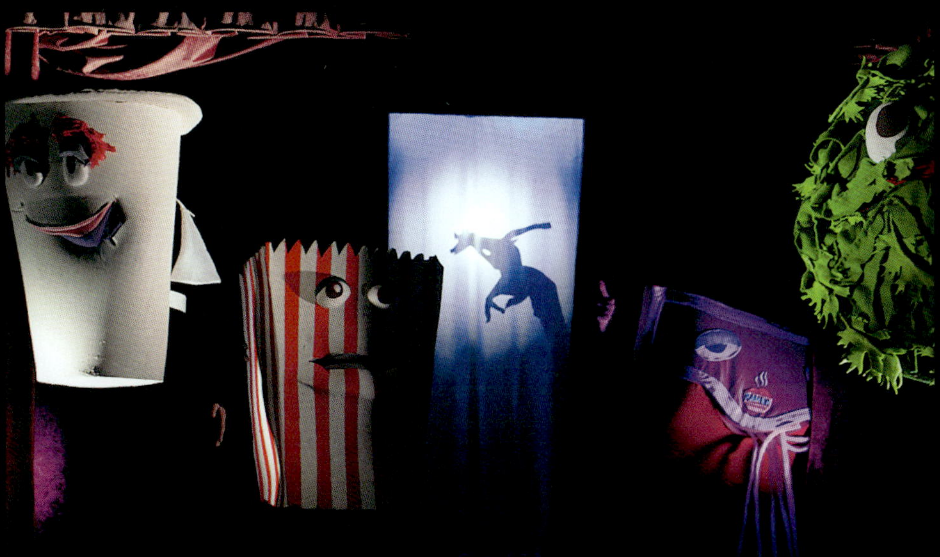

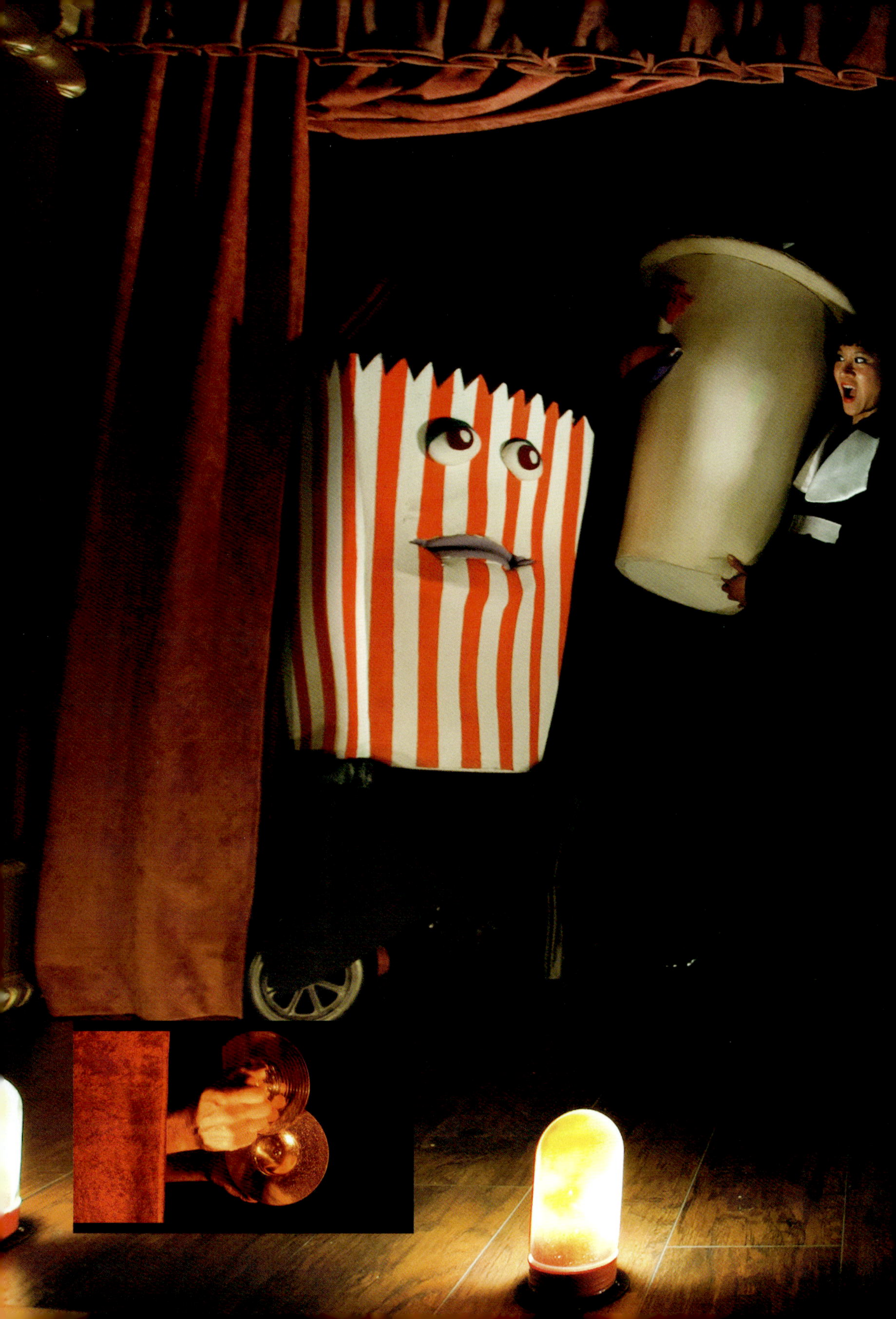

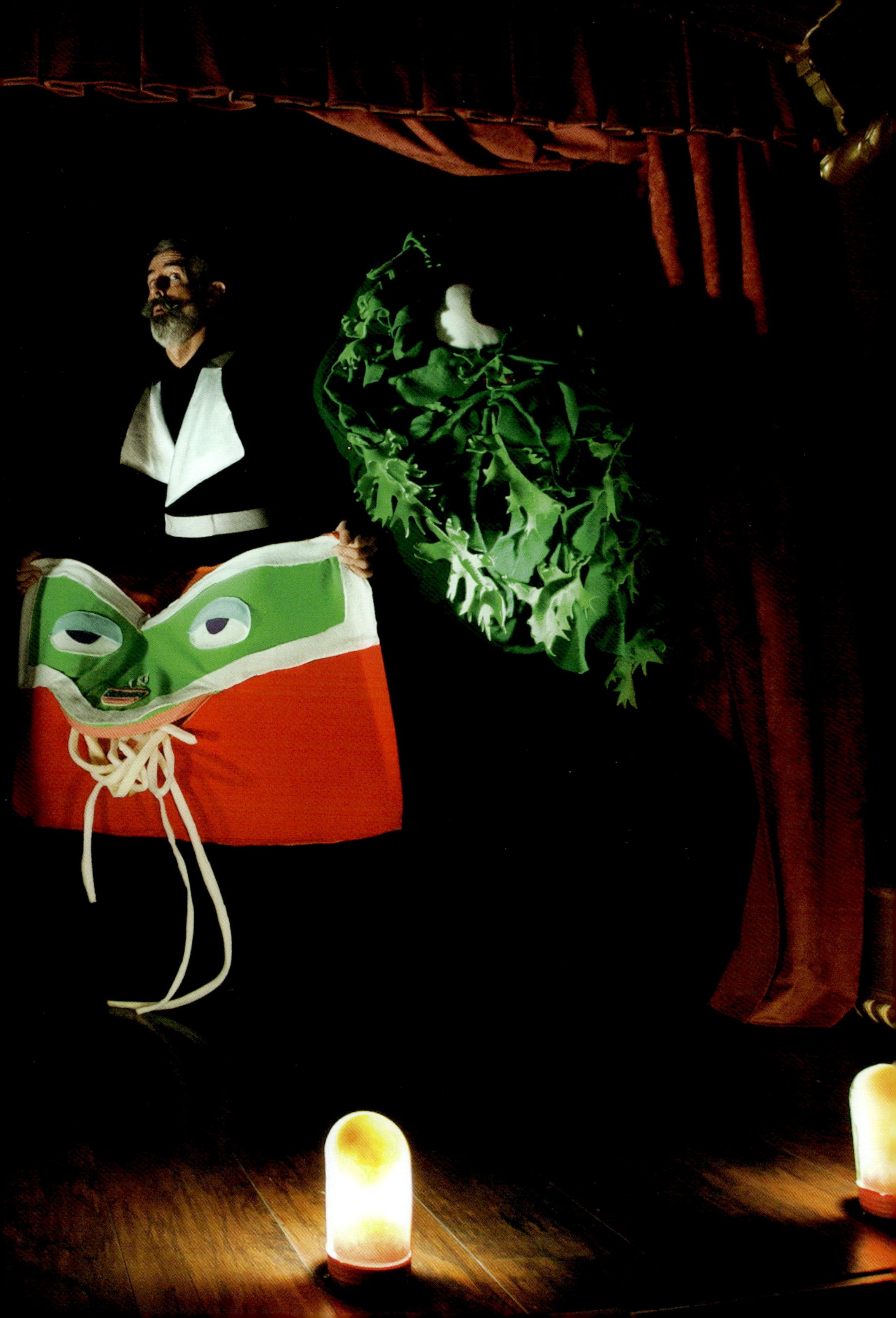

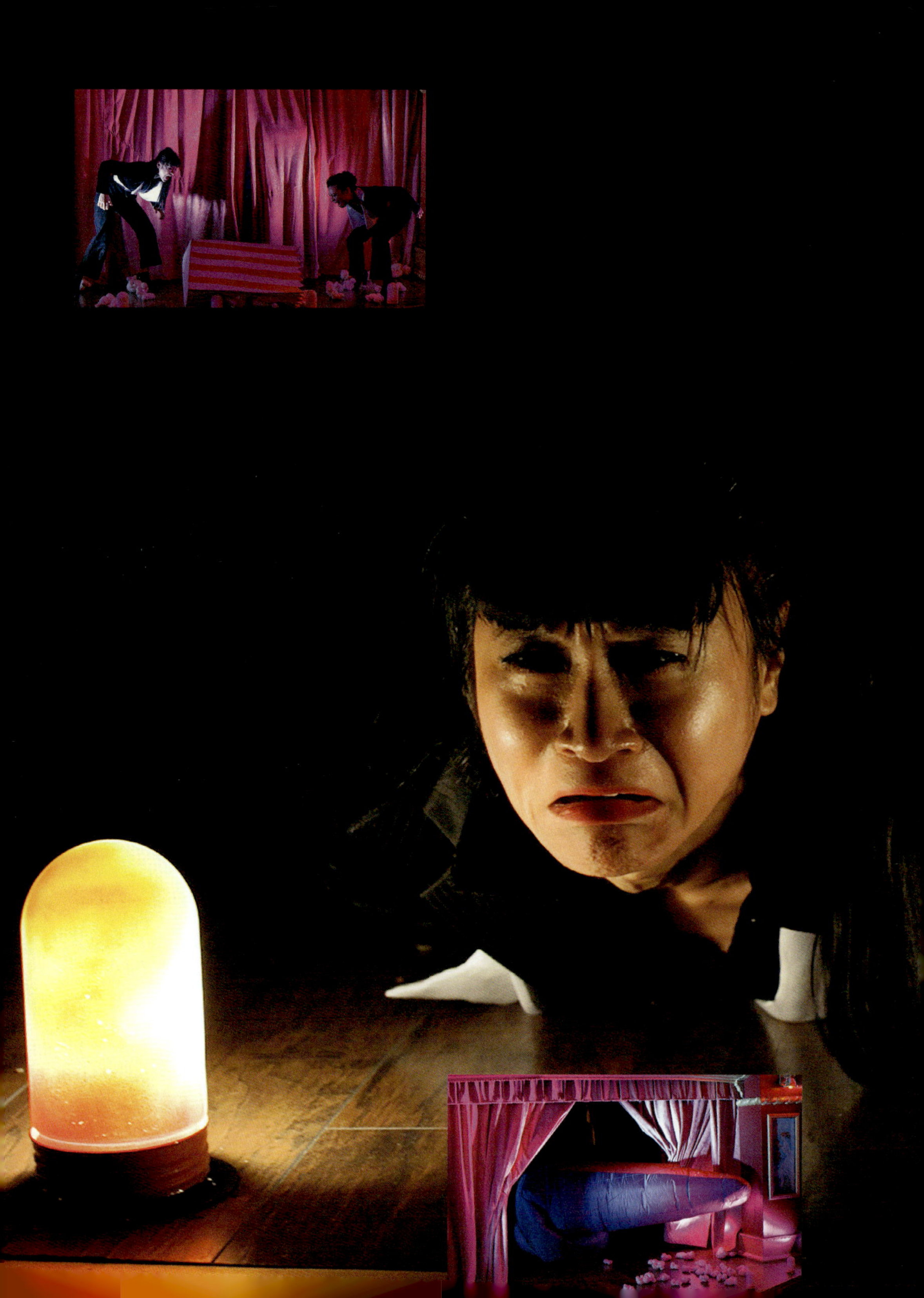

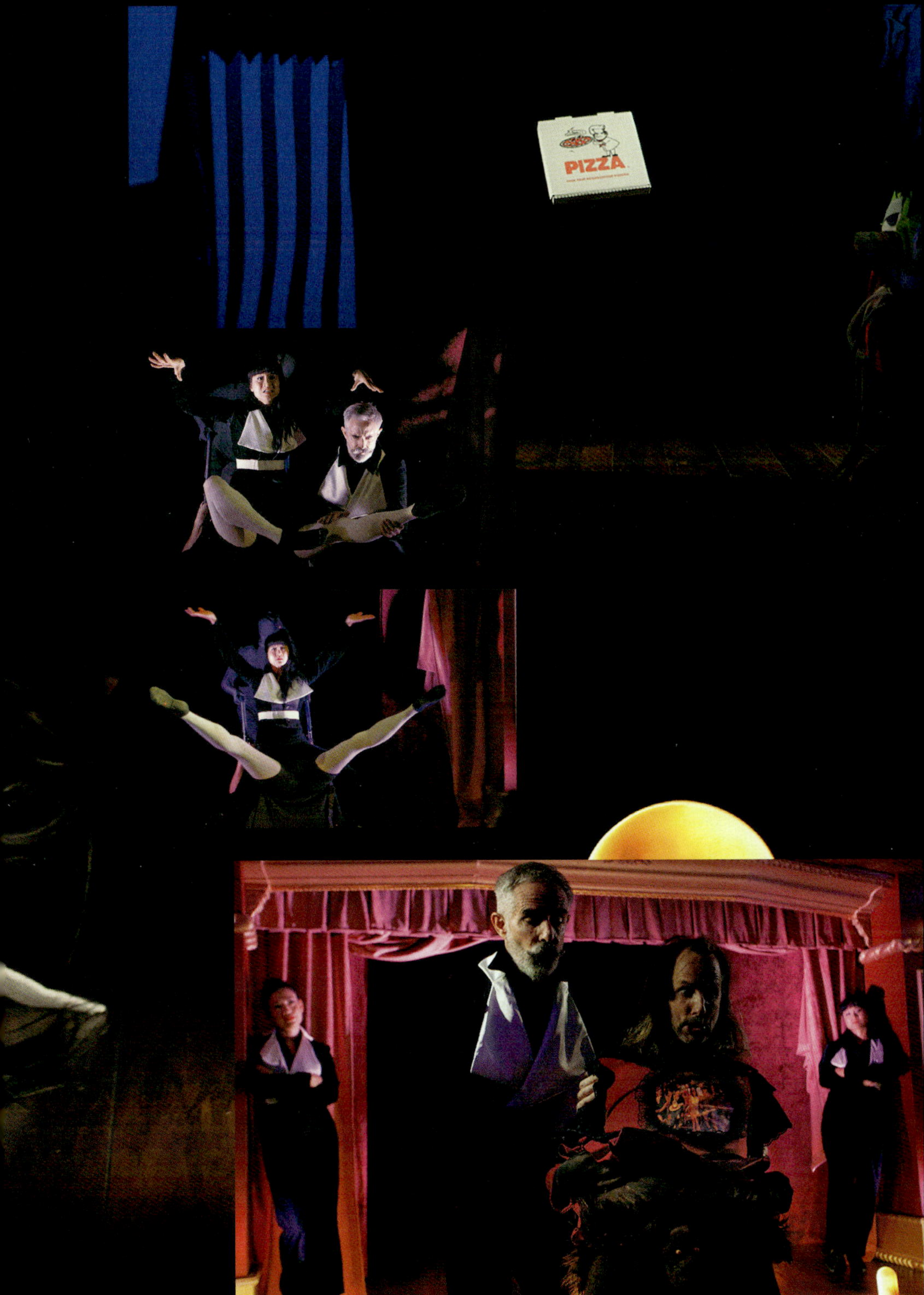
PIZZA

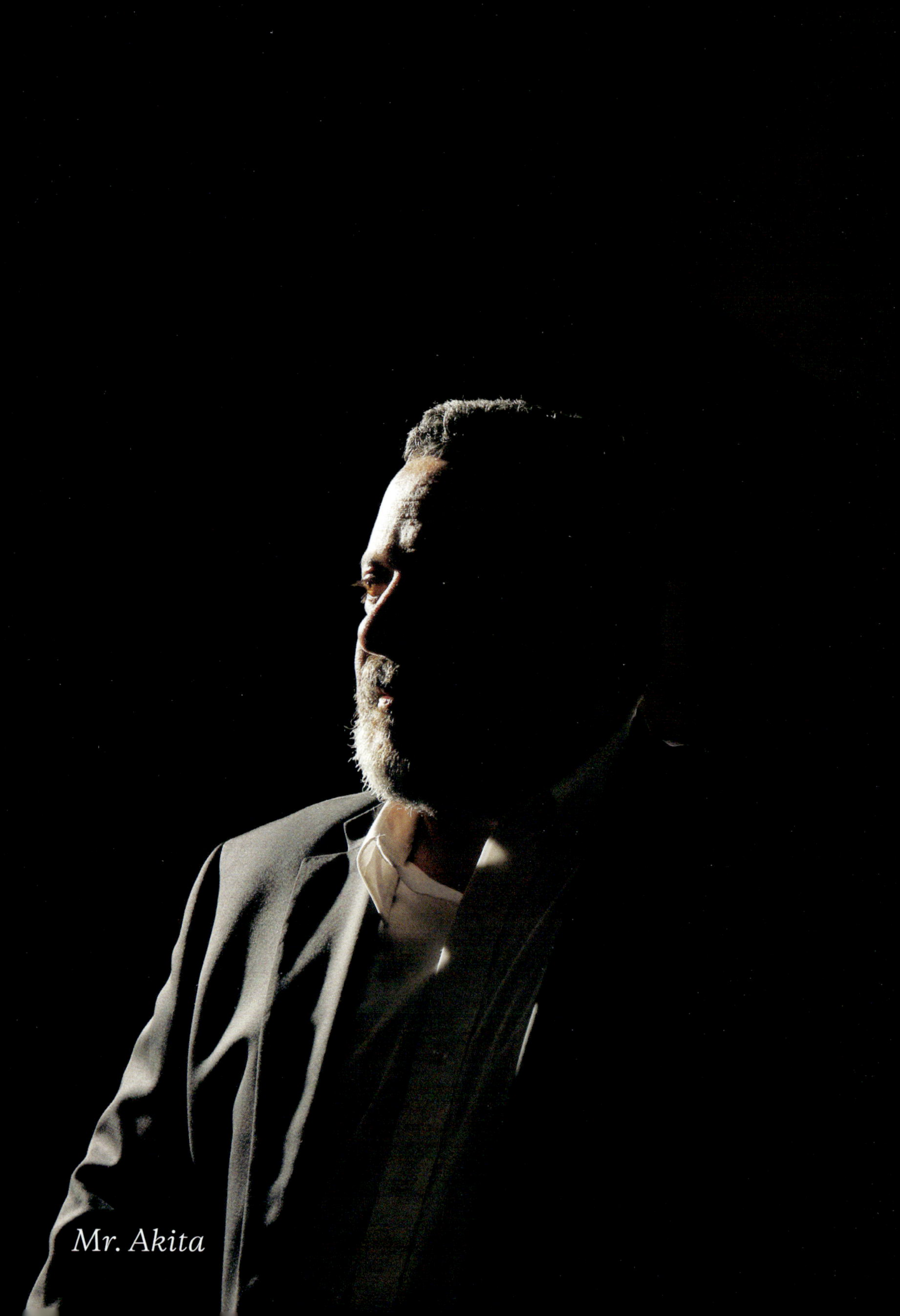

*Mr. Akita*

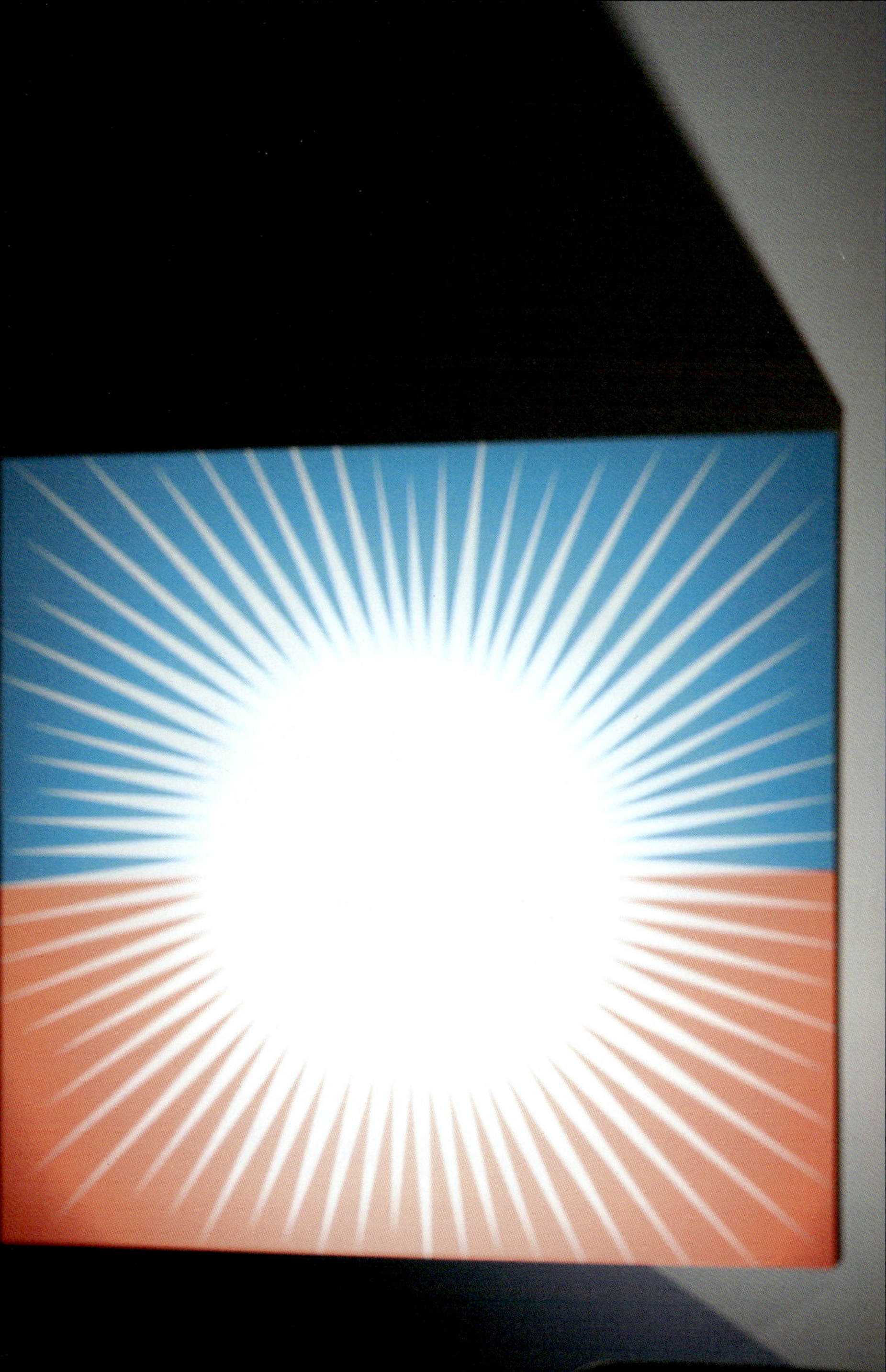

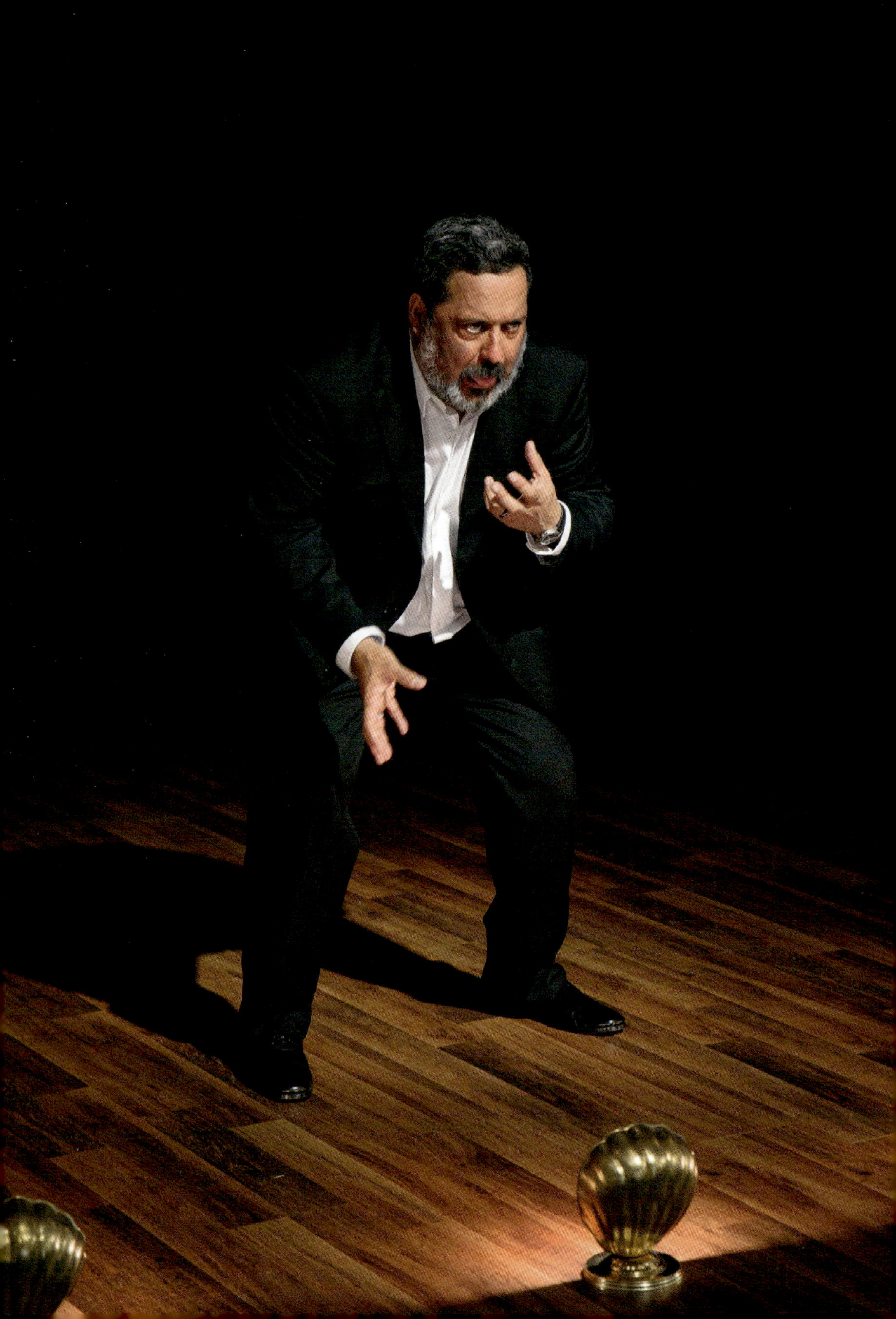

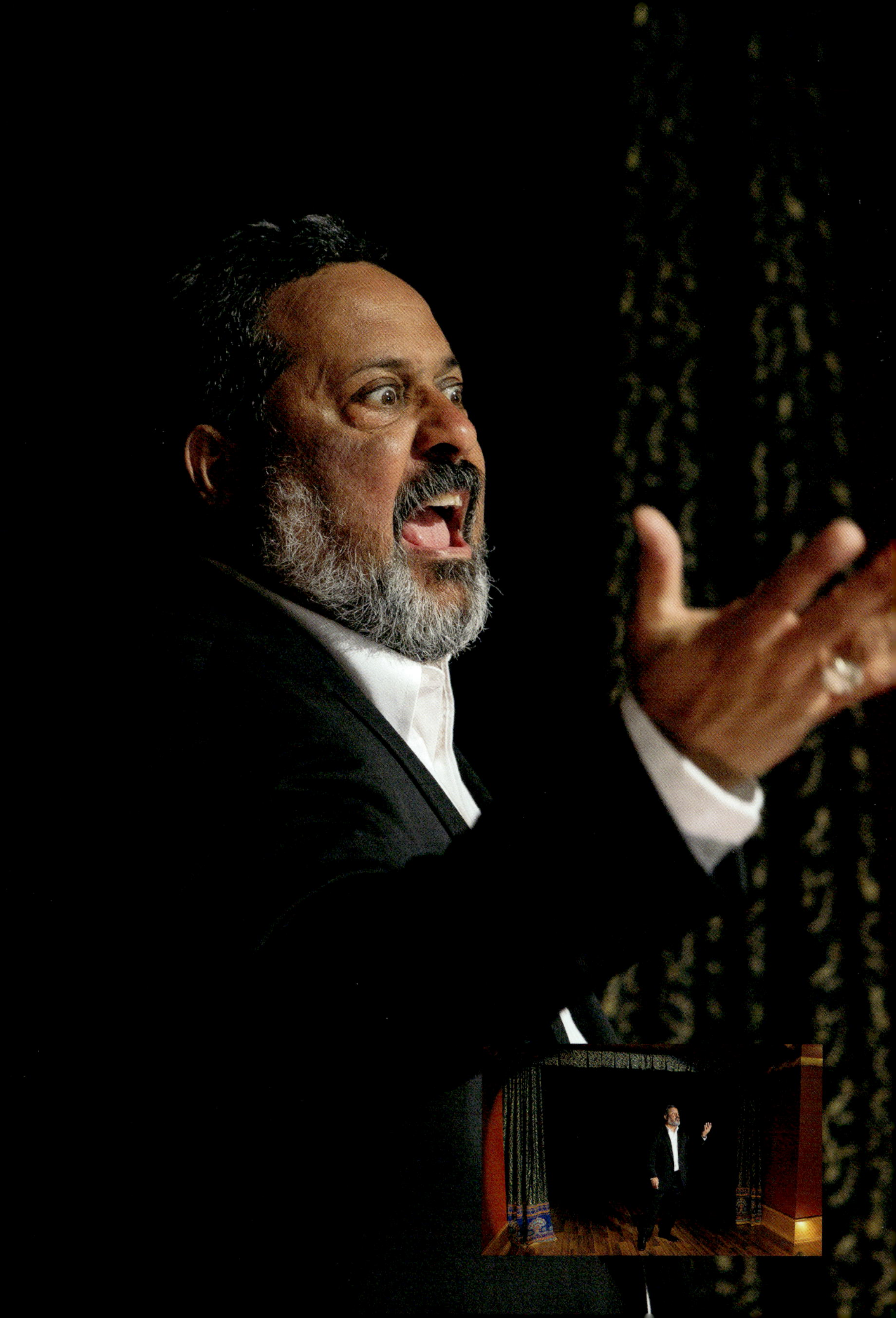

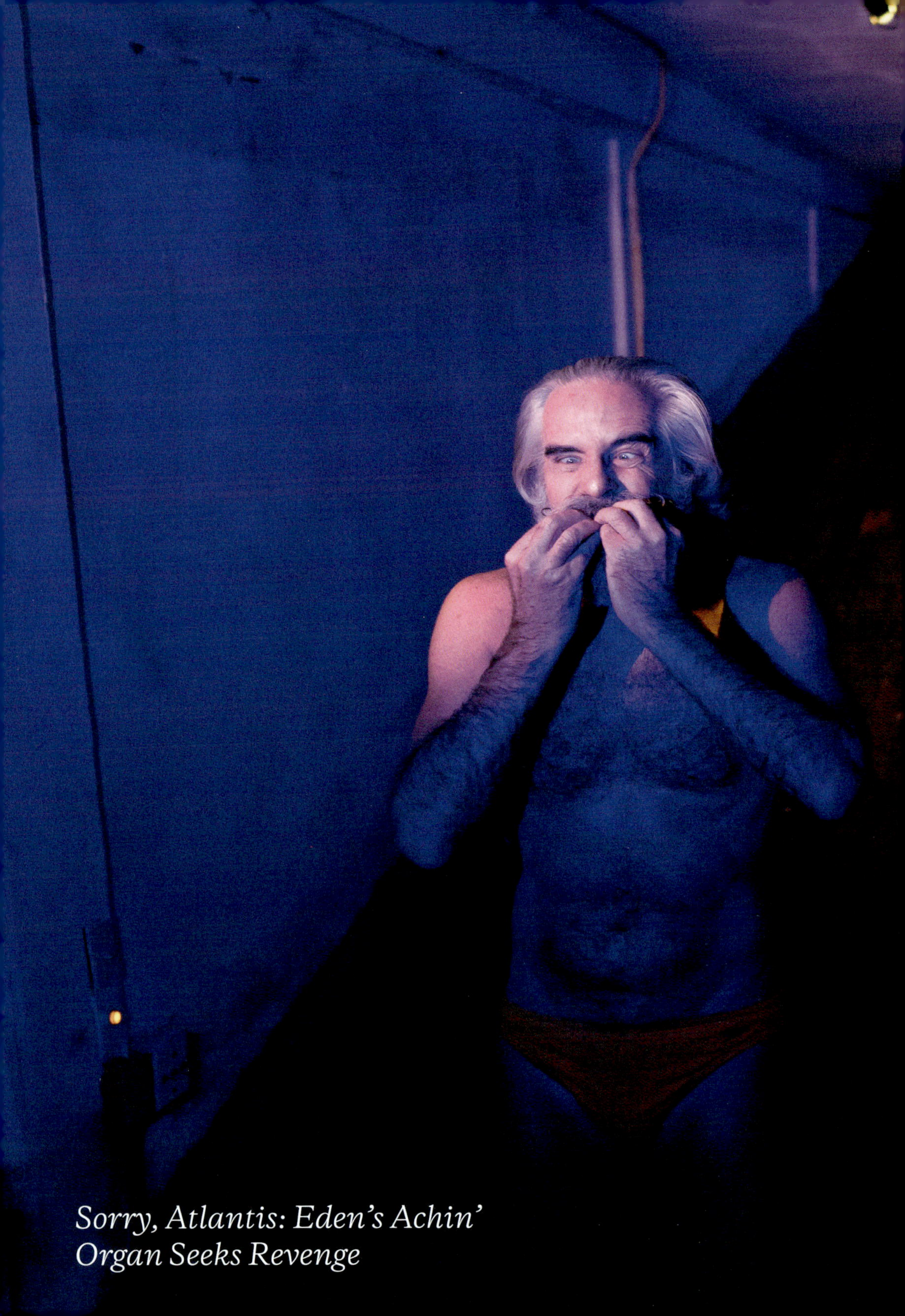

*Sorry, Atlantis: Eden's Achin' Organ Seeks Revenge*

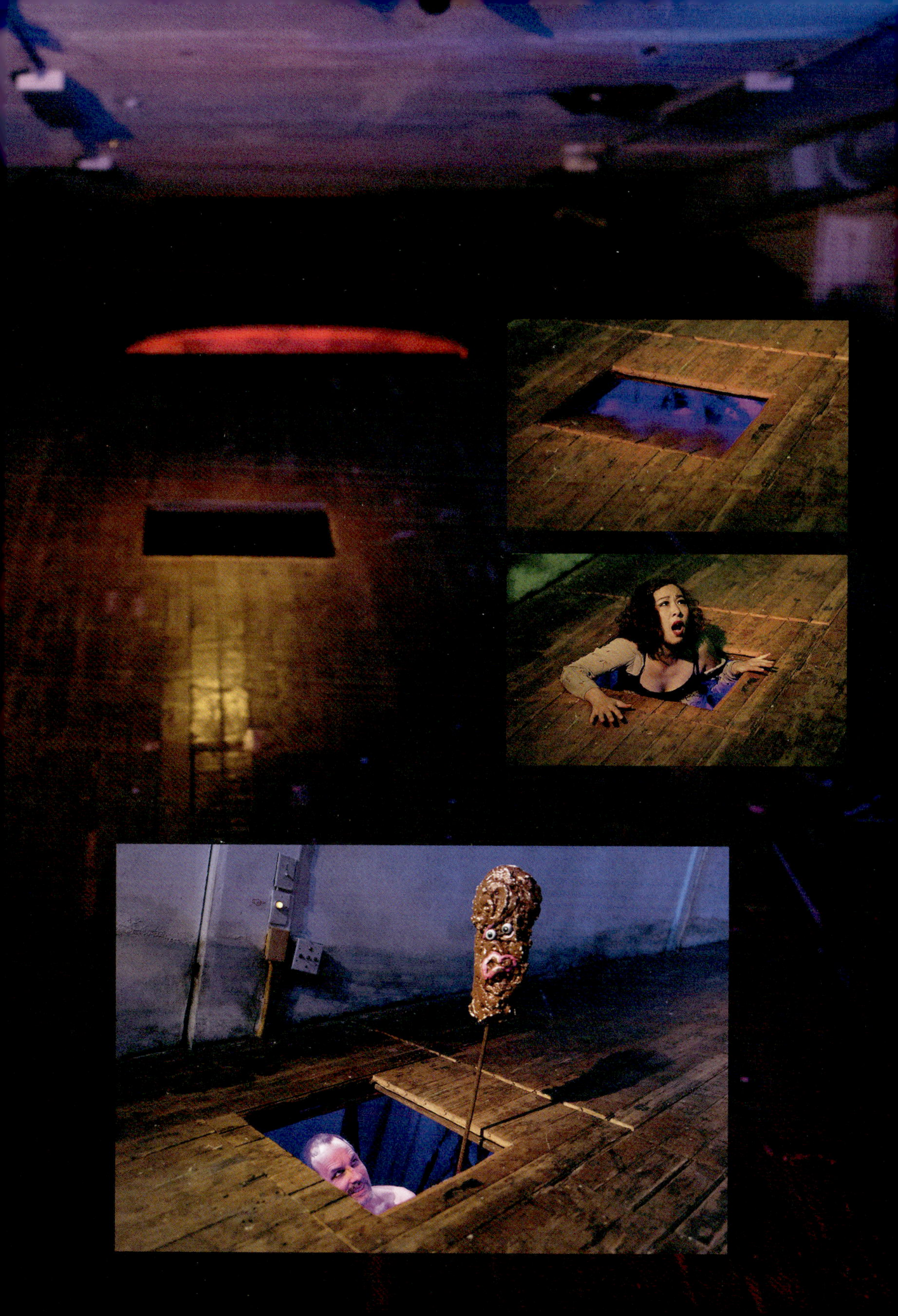

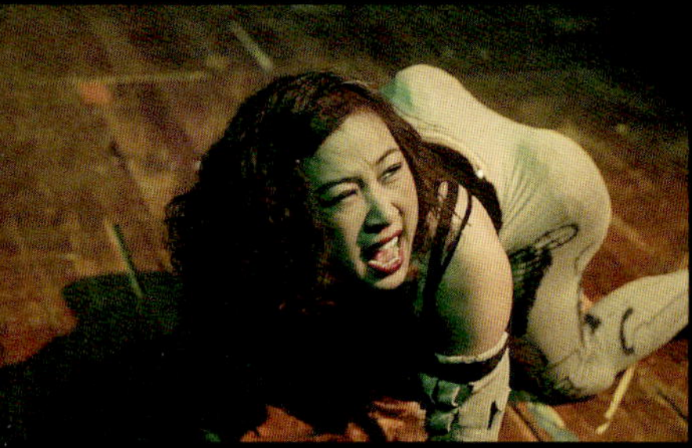
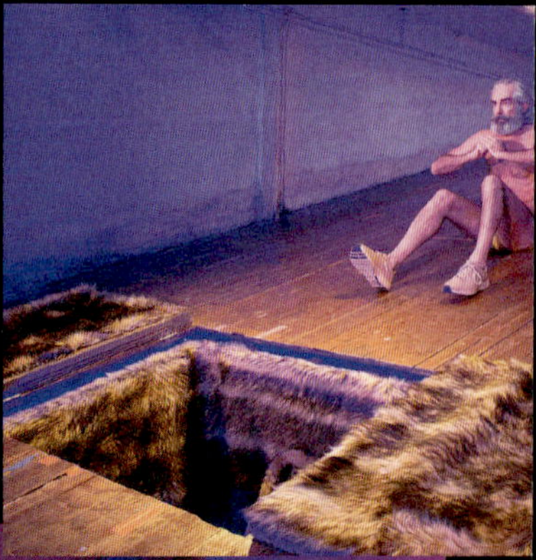
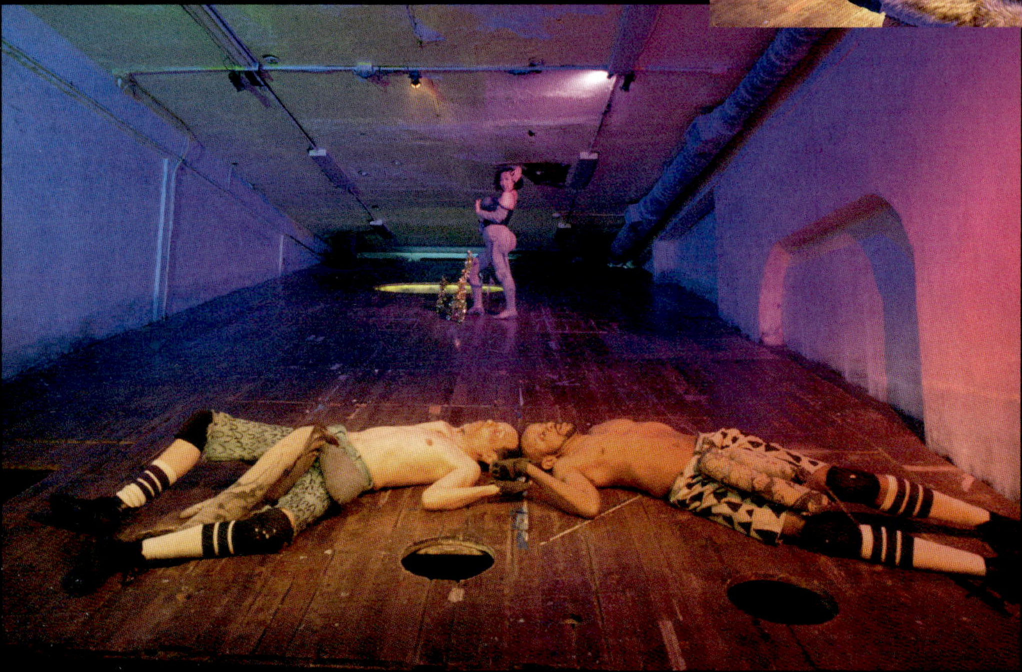
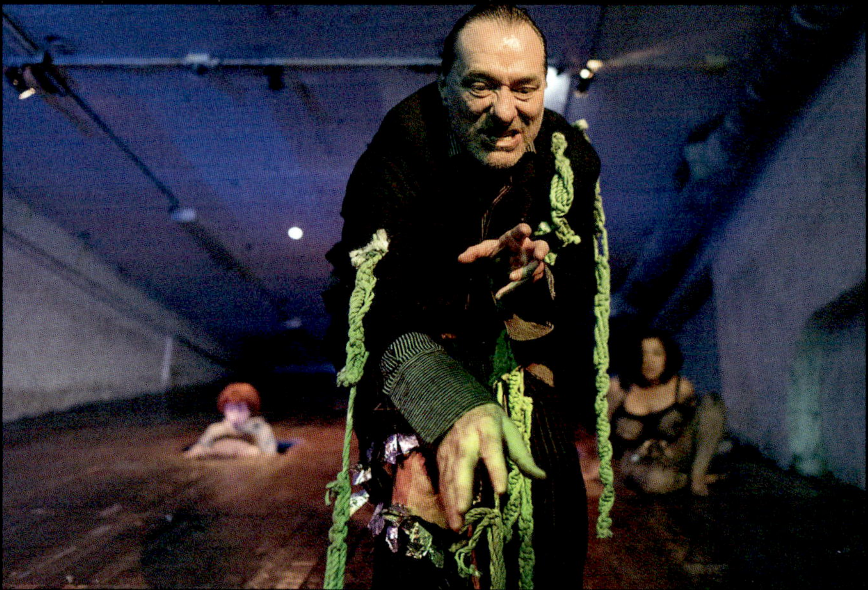

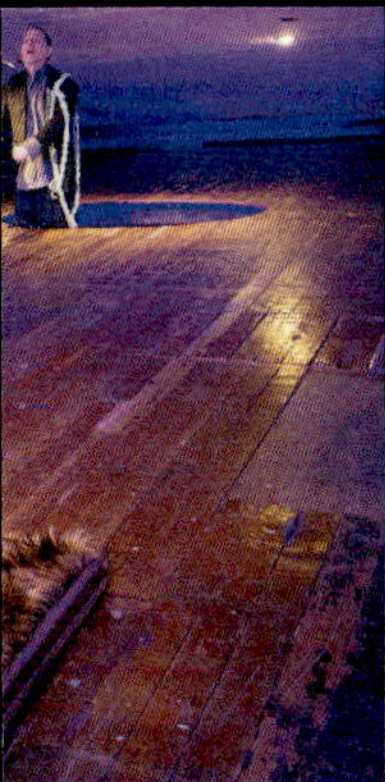

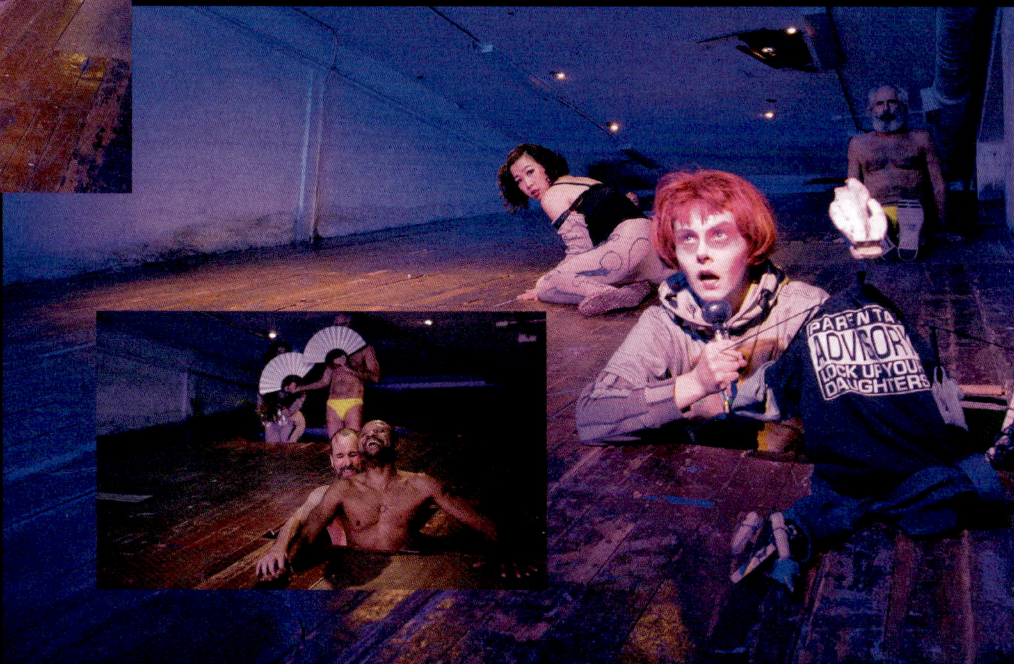
ADVISORY
LOCK UP YOUR
DAUGHTERS

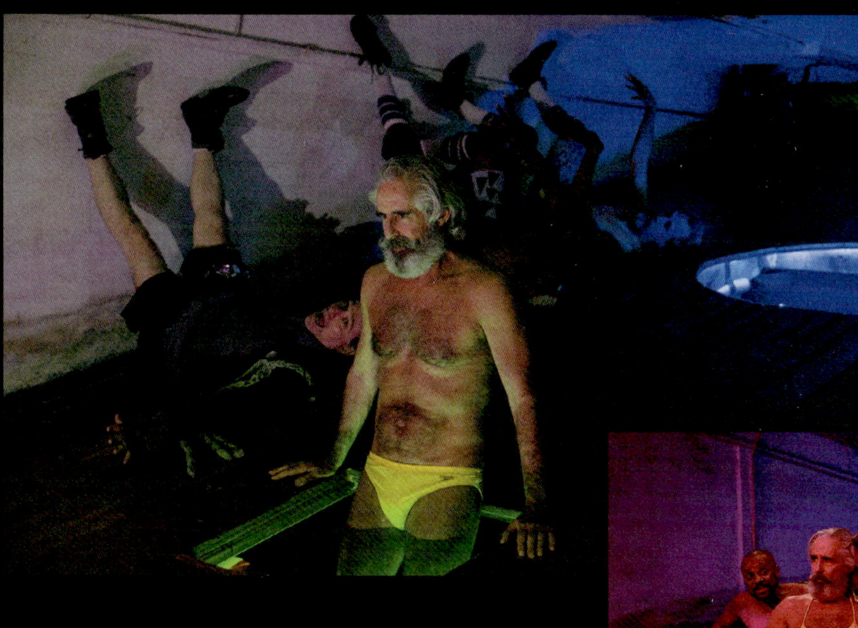

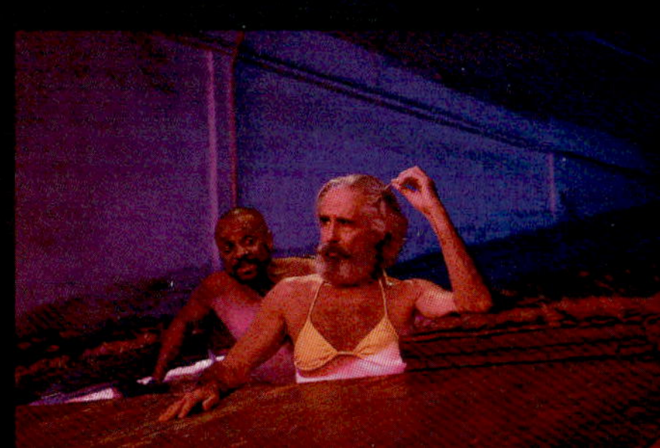

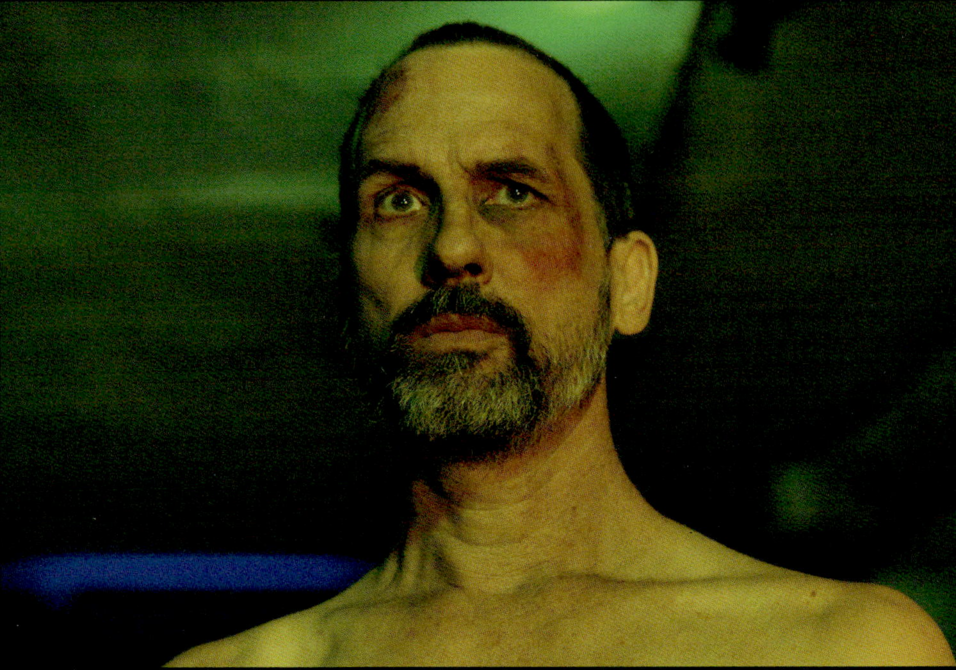

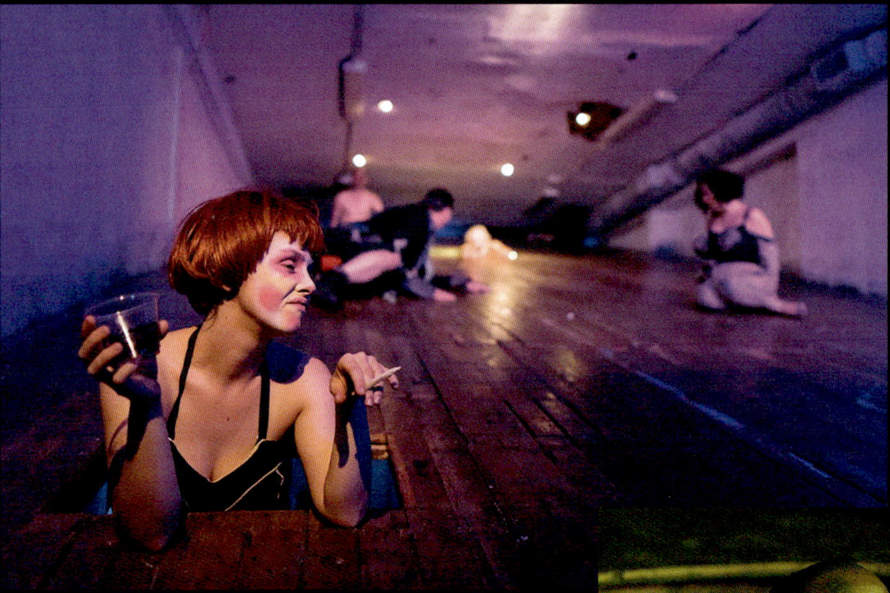

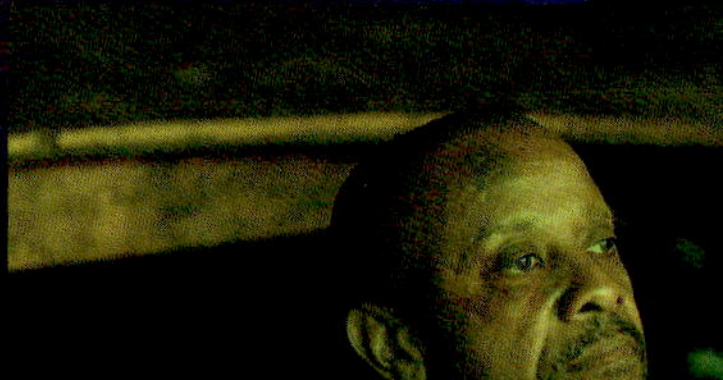

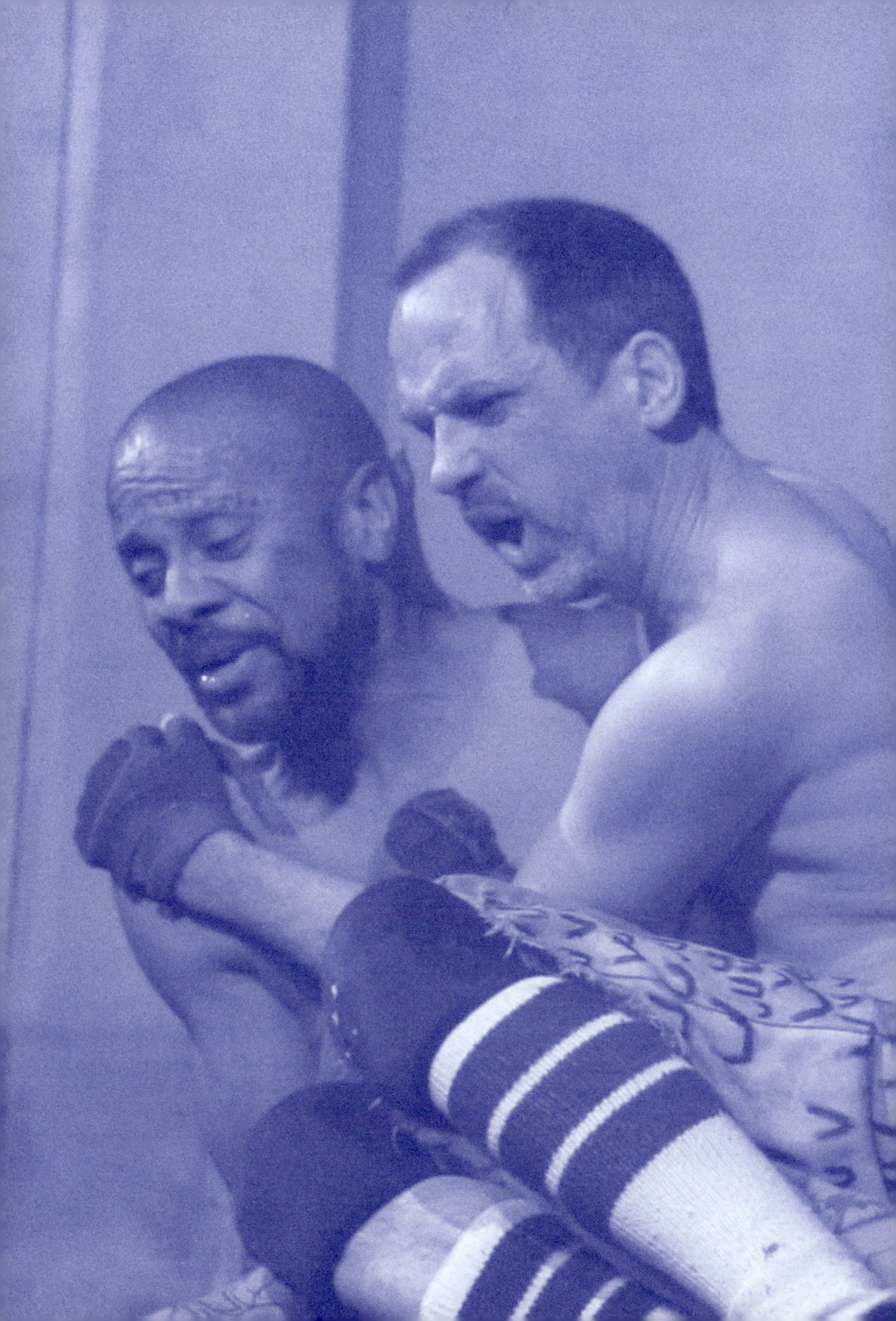

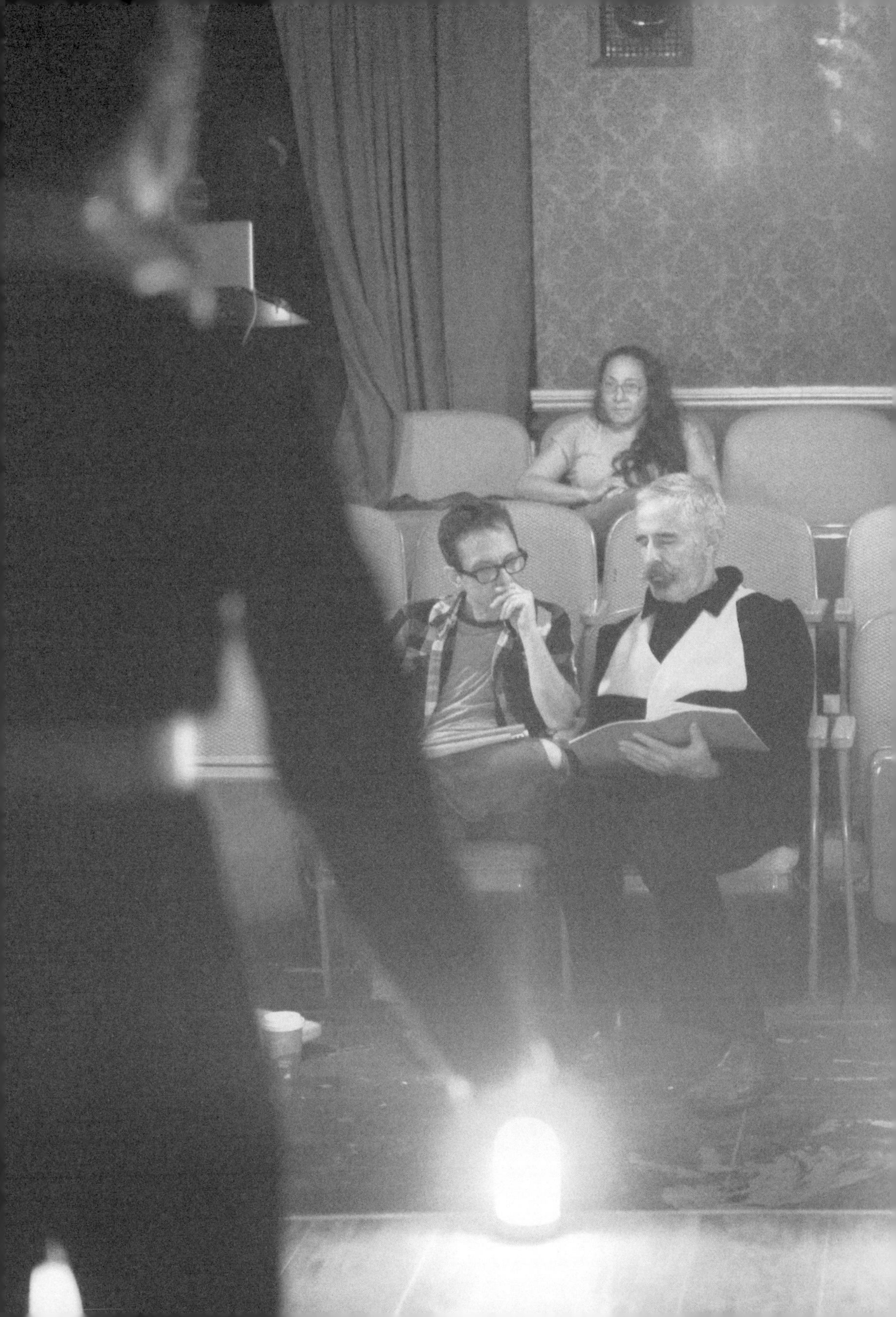

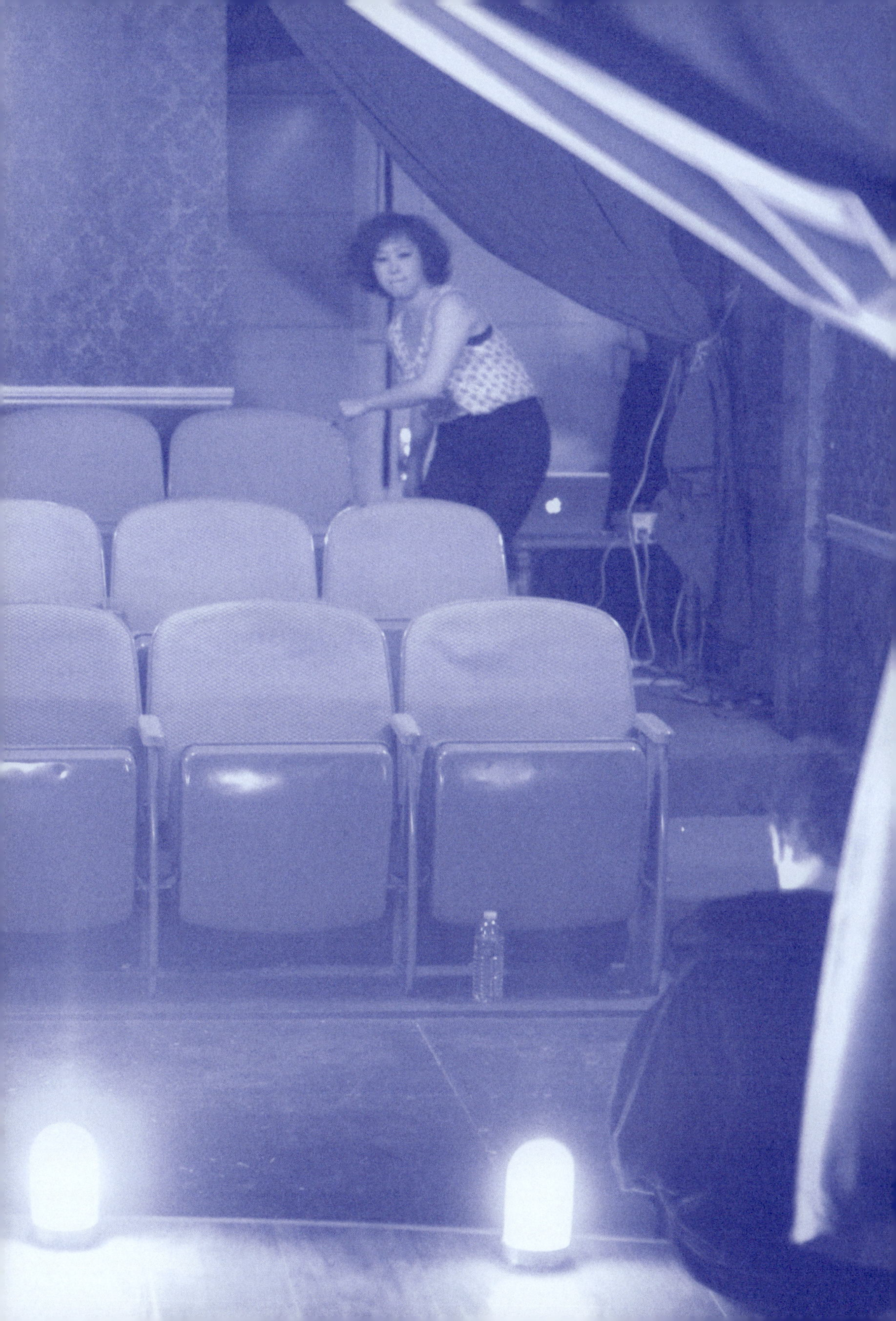

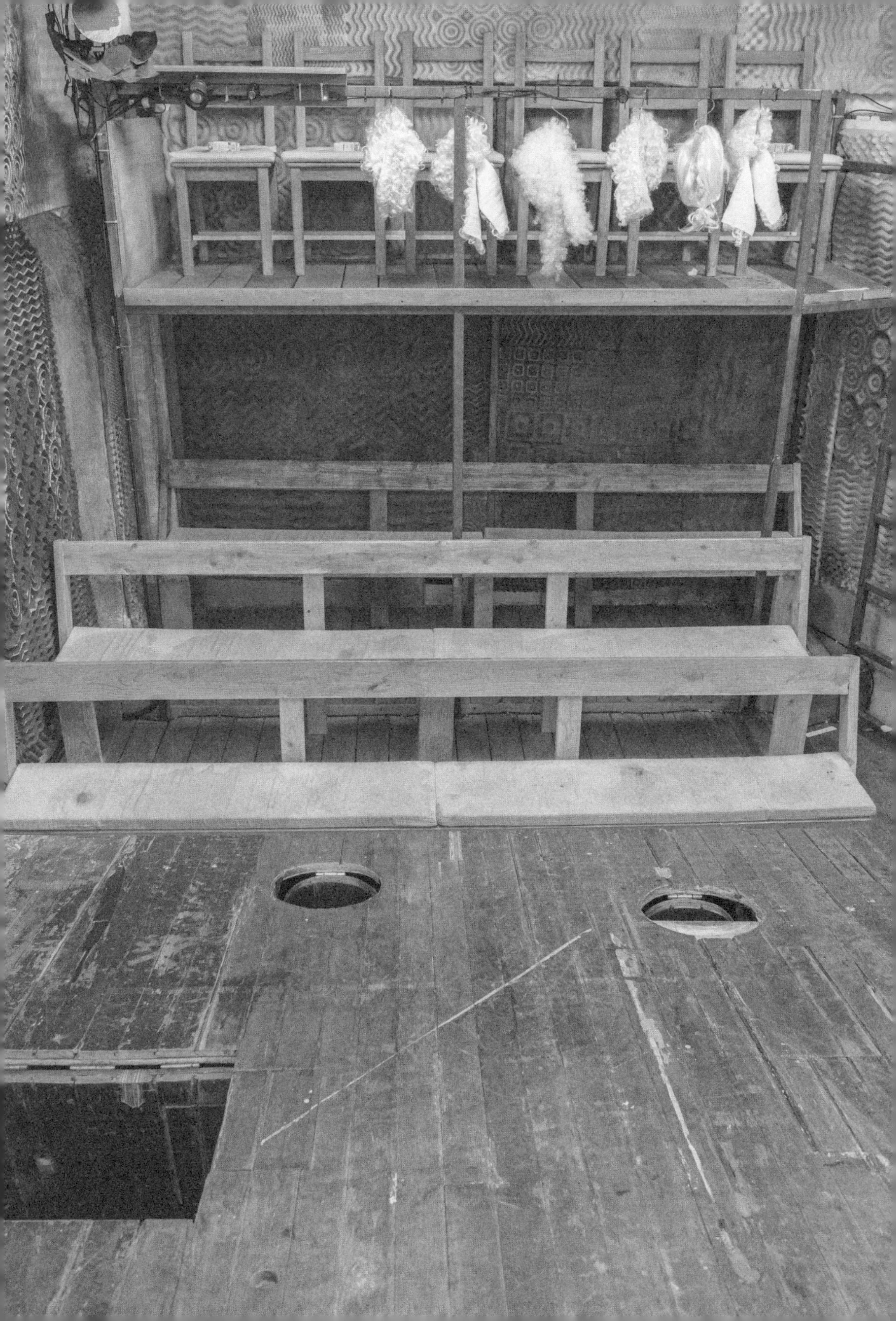

# Asher Hartman, Mark Allen, and Tim Reid in Conversation

Bartender says:
See the hole in the back of this bar?
And the paintings looked and saw the
coral sands, the ochre sands ...
the golden sands ... and the aqua ...
Pure silence.
—Man, *Mr. Akita*

**TIM** Let's start with *Mr. Akita*. That teacher Cliff Hengst plays feels hauntingly familiar. When you went to art school, Asher, did you have that guy?

**ASHER** When I decided I'd become an artist, I went to UC extension courses for painting. I met that stereotypical coffee-carrying, Thai stick-smoking older guy who was always a little bit high, trying to get the balance of coffee and weed just right ... I also had a *wonderful* painting teacher. She came in and the first thing she said to us was, "Ugh, so tired. I face-planted on the beach all night. I was drunk and fell asleep. I still have sand on my face." She'd say, "Don't be an artist. It's the worst thing you can do to yourself." She probably came into *Akita* a bit too.

**MARK** Cliff doesn't just play the teacher, though—he's also the student.

**ASHER** I've been a teacher and a student. I guess I'm in there some. I love painting and that love—from someone who tried to paint, but didn't have a career in painting—informs the writing. Like

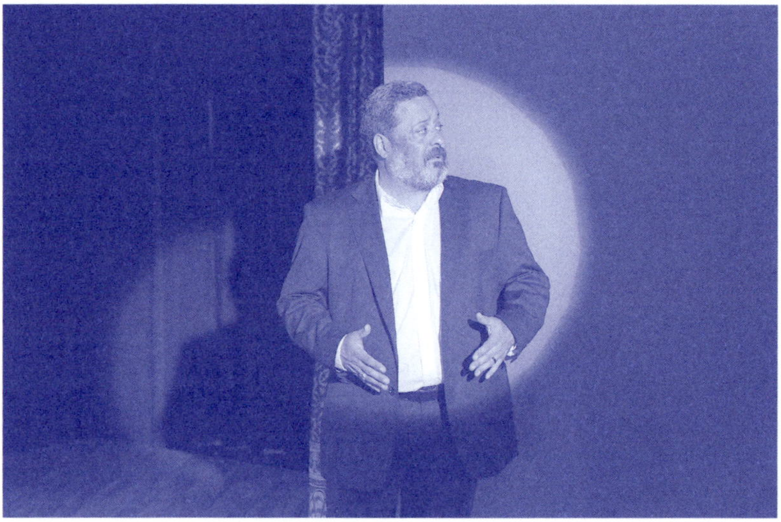

Performance view, *Mr. Akita*, Tang Teaching Museum, Skidmore College, Saratoga Springs, New York, 2015; Man (Cliff Hengst)

many artists, I've desperately wanted to be part of a club I don't want to join. I've been both alienated by and part of the art world. But really I wrote the play for Cliff.

**TIM** Talk more about Cliff.

**ASHER** Cliff is a painter, performance artist, DJ, actor, and comedian. We met through Mark, at a Machine Project retreat. I remember Cliff doing his Whitesnake routine in a dilapidated barn, volumes of bird shit on the beams above. We were all choking with laughter. That weekend he also gave a heartbreaking account of working at Walgreens in San Francisco during the AIDS crisis. Mark had already shown me a video of Cliff singing "I Left My Heart in San Francisco" into a megaphone, trying to get up a torturous hill in that city, where I was born, that I now loathe. I thought, "I gotta work with this guy or I'll be so jealous of him, I'll hate him."

**TIM** The first time I saw one of your plays, I thought, ah, you're taking these individual actors, and you're developing them, you're writing through them.

**MARK** And when I try to describe your plays to people, I say the first thing to know is that the actors will play multiple characters, sometimes in the same breath.

**ASHER** I can't write specific characters who exhibit a singular sense of self, because in every person there are many people. We are supposed to imagine ourselves as consistent, singular, whole, but we are often unaware of the many shifting parts that constitute that whole. I feel that our bodies are temporary hosts for many energies that pass through us. People are extraordinarily complex.

**TIM** This is where your practice as an intuitive comes in?

**ASHER** In my psychic practice, I often have the experience of stepping into another's energy. There is cloak of feeling that seems to come over me. It's similar to acting, where there is the experience of inhabiting someone who is not there. Feelings, ways of being, affect, will enter me temporarily.

**MARK** I'd like to hear how that happened in writing *Mr. Akita*. I mean, Cliff plays the Man, but how many personas are involved, and how did you and Cliff find them?

**ASHER** Well, the play deals with my own ideals of masculinity, which I could not match, and ideals of painting beyond my grasp. I would write a lot, I'd visit Cliff, we would work on pieces of the play, and then more would come. Mr. Akita took on many personas as we looked for him, and one morning as he was shifting from longshoreman to '80s New Yorker, Cliff's parents' Dutch accents arrived. That Mr. Akita was a dog was certain, but what kind of dog hadn't been clear. I think when Cliff began living in this Dutch persona, it became clear to us that Mr. Akita was de Kooning.

**TIM** So you'll take from an actor's way of speaking and develop the lines from there. The words have to carry a certain musicality, built on top of physicality, on top of affect, on top of psychic work.

**ASHER** Yeah, I start with the actor's cadence and affect. Then something of who they are, or might be, something hidden, appears.

The actor builds on that. We start questioning and refining, and we undergo a long process of internal discovery.

**TIM** Each line is refined through rehearsal after rehearsal. Once the lines are written out and given to the actors, there's a process of sharing what's been written, seeing what lands and what doesn't. Then, in the end, onstage, nothing is improvised.

**ASHER** I feel like a writer whose work is enacted. In my limited experience in attempting to "craft" a play, I get bored, so I'm uncomfortable with the idea that I'm a playwright. I know that I want to write plays that are emotionally exhilarating, like music, or like abstract painting—the writing of *Akita* also came from Emily Joyce's painting, *Sun Burn (Split) 1*.

**MARK** If there was an elevator pitch for this play, it might be: Macho comedian talks to delicate painting.

**TIM** There's a lot of tension in that setup, in how much we desire to say. *Mr. Akita* is, after all, a forty-five-minute-long monologue.

**MARK** The long-on-talk teacher is funny in part because *Akita* was written with art students in mind as the audience—we produced it first at the Tang Museum at Skidmore College.

**ASHER** Few students attended. That a play made for students about their intended career went unattended felt perfect—art imitating life.

**TIM** Later you were asked to perform *Akita* at Berkeley Art Museum, and then at a blue-chip art gallery, at Hauser & Wirth in LA. Your audience is, for the most part, members of the art world.

**ASHER** Yes. With *Akita* it was important for me to address my antipathy toward those spaces where class and power are so salient and ripe for challenge—museums and universities. I don't know if it's relevant, but I'm a trans man raised by a very macho and complicated guy. I was fascinated by men and masculinity as a kid. Strangely, I worried about the draft. Once I was an adult, my dad would call me occasionally to tell me to get my prostate checked, and when I told him on the phone that I didn't have a prostate, there'd always be this confused silence on the other end. The masculinity I loved—the "tough guy" or the joker—connects to a class identification that gets challenged in these spaces that keep most people out.

**TIM** This irreducible thing you're putting before the audience, it was Cliff's ability as a performer to marshal it.

**ASHER** The actors make so much happen. They have to get into, and on top of, complex spoken language—its volume, pitch, consonants, and vowels squeeze and attack our sense of desire. I see language as a way to negotiate the unseen, to try to describe the outlines of what can't actually be articulated.

> The theater is
> A shit factory for beginners.
> —Vital Organ,
> *Purple Electric Play (PEP!)*

**ASHER** When I'm writing I often go into a light trance. I feel an odd sensation in my body (which I also get when I eat yogurt). I'm not sure if there are spirits at all, if specific spirits are speaking to me, if I'm not merely addressing my unconscious … but when I'm in that state, I know something useful is happening. I have very little interest in the day-to-day. Not to put it down, but trying to understand relationships, character motivations, is of very little interest. I want passages that seem to come from another place. So if events are illogical, if they "make no sense" on the surface, I trust that they make sense in another, less obvious way.

**MARK** I remember when you wrote *Purple Electric Play*, you just sat in the basement theater at Machine Project for weeks, typing nonstop.

**ASHER** Yes, well, I was a little freaked out because while I was writing, spirits—or my unconscious mind—would say: "No mercy," "Step it up," "You have to be cruel!" I would look down at my keyboard to see that I had written that. They insisted that I not spare *the left*, which, of course, is maybe too common now, the critique. The language of *PEP!* is dense, and the scenes are layered with quickly shifting meanings and allegiances as the actors move through arch exchanges between bitter vaudevillians and "up with the people" pro-peace dance numbers. Theater's historical role as enemy and friend of political change is the larger subject of the play, which was inspired by readings of the French Revolution.

**MARK** *Purple Electric Play* felt secretive, enclosed, nefarious, a little poisonous. It was completely removed from the world. Even before the play started, you had to walk so far to get down into the theater.

**ASHER** That theater that you built, Mark, with a bunch of other artists in the bowels of Machine was a little jewel—just seventeen seats, and basically Marie Antoinette's private theater in Versailles as seen through a kind of Las Vegas lounge-meets-Russian Constructivist lens. We aimed for a blacklight theater full of illusions, where objects or body parts seemed to float free of supports. Things happen in the dark that are a little bit sour, but entertaining, frightening, and cheap, where you're not sure of the actors' intentions. They're constantly reassuring you, glibly.

**MARK** We used everything everywhere. We put a trap in the ceiling for the boot to come down. We used the resonance of footsteps above. Whenever people used the restroom, you heard the flush. Lucas Wrench was working at Machine then, and his desk station upstairs was incorporated into the play—he was there playing hangman before the show, talking on the phone in the middle.

**ASHER** I loved what Lucas did. When you looked at what he was drawing, sitting at his desk as the bored gallery assistant, it was actually horrifying. The violence was a little too emphatic. He was a little too involved in his murderous game.

**TIM** So the idea of bloody revolution—not just the French Revolution—energized you?

**ASHER** Well, I was fascinated by Robespierre's role in it—how an idealistic but perhaps personally troubled person became the orchestrator of the Terror. Outside of any straightforward reading of a quest for power, I'm interested in how it is that we delude ourselves about our purposes, how ideology can inspire and ruin us.

**MARK** The play is way broader in its references than late-eighteenth-century France.

**ASHER** Yes, I was also drawn to the aesthetics of revolution in the 1960s and '70s. In particular, how quickly it became corporate fashion, like the peace symbol. I was thinking, too, about Raffaella Carra's jaw-dropping dance number with Adriano

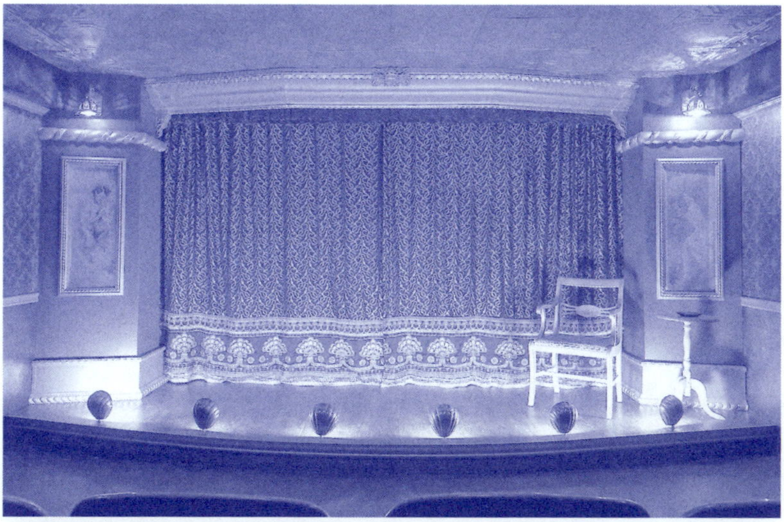

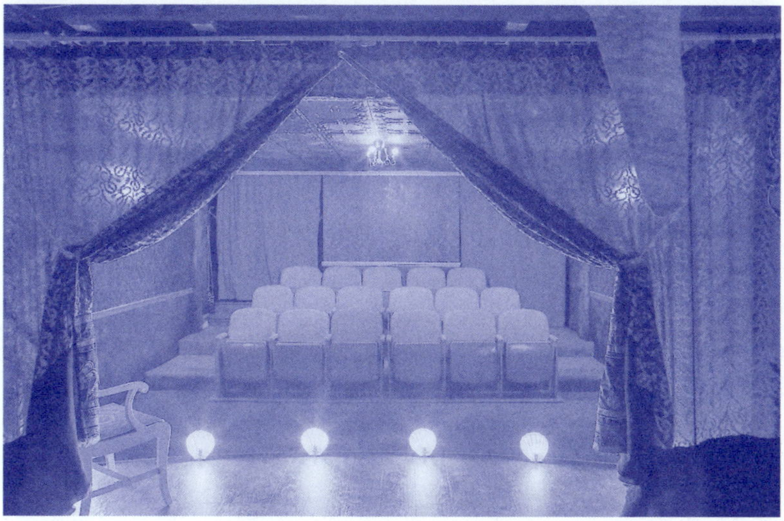

Magic Theater, basement of Machine Project, Los Angeles, 2014

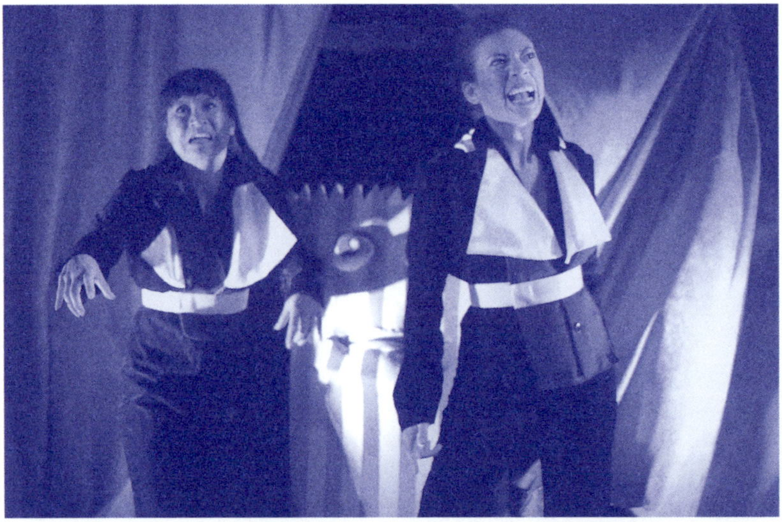

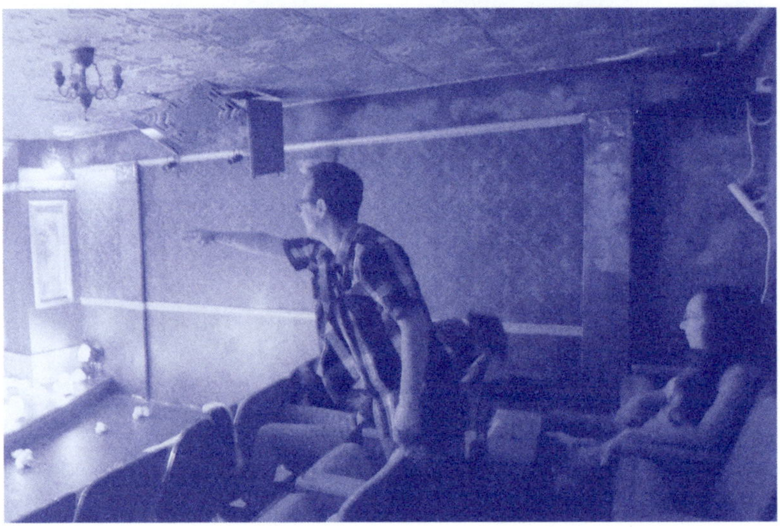

Rehearsal views, *Purple Electric Play (PEP!)*, Machine Project, Los Angeles, 2014; (above) from left: Vital Organ (Jasmine Orpilla), Donkey, and Vital Organ II (Kalean Ung); (below) from left: Asher Hartman and Carol Guidry (choreographer)

Celentano, "Prisencolinensinainciusol" (which is a pretty trenchant critique of American culture), and those mild skits with puppets advocating "peace" with gentle Alan Alda-like men—about their juxtaposition against the understanding that theater and entertainment may in fact be purposefully malicious. As the characters state, "Jesters are by nature cruel." I wondered what it would be like to talk in code about political violence to my audience of culture makers. I wondered if they would be able to recognize their own allegiances and ambivalences in the characters' political positions as they slide around the edges of radicalism toward the cautious, conditioned middle.

**MARK** And *PEP!* really was so much of its moment. In the script there's that brief stage direction that mentions a Pitbull mask. In the performance, an actor walked onstage as a rapper who was huge then, in 2014. I worry that the plays published as a book can't capture all the synchronies of the performances ...

**ASHER** There was so much happening so fast, way beyond language in this play. It's definitely hard to convey in book form.

**TIM** You implicate us, the audience, in having an actor play the role of the Audience. He's kind of the ultimate buffoon.

**ASHER** Joe Seely plays the Audience both as a literal clown, full of pathos and vitriol, and as a dude who killed someone during a robbery in a liquor store in a fit of rage. In my experience, there is an audience-performer contract that says "I won't hurt you if you don't hurt me." That contract is seldom broken in conventional, polite theater, but often is on the street. Because the artist is vulnerable and the audience is potentially violent—as the mob—I think the actor must possess a certain disdain for the audience, and distance, as opposed to the cloying need for approval that is so understandable but so damaging to theater.

**MARK** We can't forget about the puppets.

**ASHER** Talking to puppets seems like a special kind of humiliation for actors.

**TIM** The actors beat the puppet Donkey to death at the end!

**ASHER** Honestly that broke my heart. I loved Donkey. He is the popcorn puppet who seems to be an innocent bystander to all of the violence. He's in pain. He's lonely. He wants love. But he has to go.

**TIM** America's worship of innocence. It's really hard to challenge.

**ASHER** All Donkey wants is to dream, to escape. The Vital Organs are angry at the stage, at the hypnotic effect of entertainment. They want to undo what they have done as entertainers. They have to destroy Donkey. Then Mother Theater destroys them—this incredibly long, inflated Mylar puppet tongue crosses the stage into the audience to lick the spectators and punish the actors, sweeping them away. Americans tend to believe violence cleanses, even we when tell ourselves we feel otherwise, even when we imagine ourselves as pacifists. We get excited by it.

## Will you allow me a quiet death, fellas? No? Well. Ugh. Blech.
## —Poseidon, *Sorry, Atlantis: Eden's Achin' Organ Seeks Revenge*

**MARK** Undoing is how I think about *Sorry, Atlantis*, because for me it was about reaching an end. Asher, you wrote it when I asked you to do the last show before Machine closed. At that point we had nothing to lose.

**ASHER** What I remember you saying was, "I want to take the floorboards up at Machine to put them in at a thirty-degree angle. What can you do with that?"

**MARK** My original plan was to remove all the beams on the ground floor, to then flood the basement. I went as far as to talk to structural engineers, who said it couldn't be done without drawing the attention of the city. So instead we took the floor up to reinstall it as a raked stage.

**ASHER** Wow ... I didn't know about the flood idea. When I looked at the angled floor, I thought, "Oh my God, this is a jetty on the ocean. This is Grecian for sure." So I proposed a play about my parents' sex life or something.

**TIM** Mark, you left the actors with no wings, no "backstage."

**MARK** At one point we considered a Plexiglas floor, with two actors underneath, sort of stuck there, with your feet on their faces.

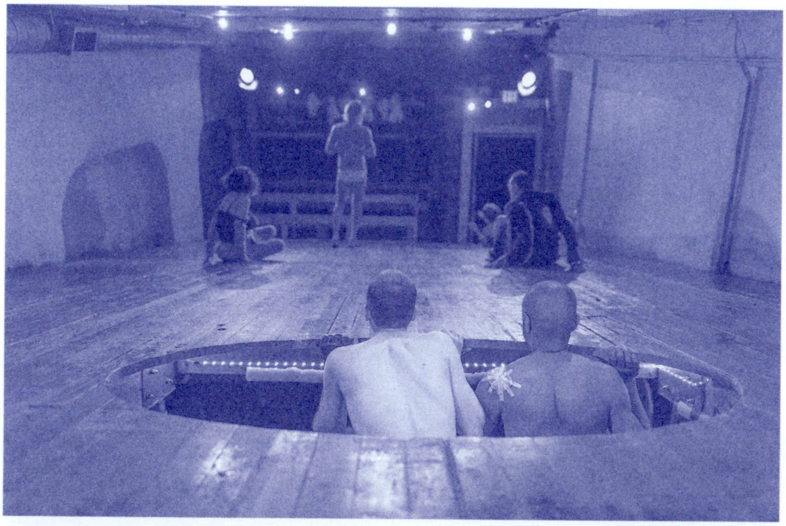

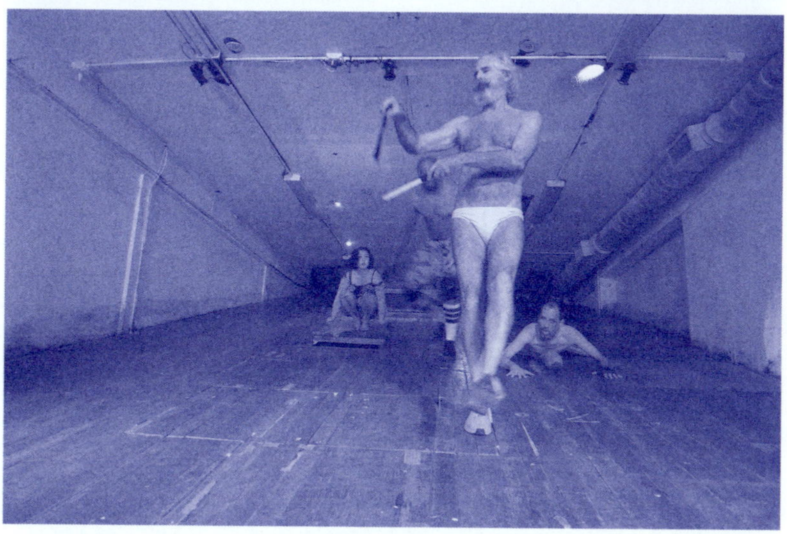

Rehearsal views, *Sorry, Atlantis: Eden's Achin' Organ Seeks Revenge*, 2017; (above) clockwise from upper left: Sledgeweed (Zut Lorz), Poseidon (Philip Littell), Freebird (Chelsea Rector), Harry Who Tomato Face (Michael Bonnabel), Po (Paul Outlaw), and Jo (Joe Seely); (below) from left: Sledgeweed, Po, Poseidon, and Jo

**ASHER** Yes, that would have been sublime. We did have a grating under the audience's feet, through which Poseidon appeared. We also cut holes in the stage, so the actors could come up from below. I worried that they couldn't walk at a thirty-degree angle for the whole play—although they often did, with striking ease.

**MARK** In the lower audience, it was like, "Where am I?" The perspective was so forced, the actors would look like giants when really close, or like little specks in the distance.

**ASHER** Yes, I wasn't aware of just how much vertigo the audience would feel in the grip of European perspective. Making plays for Machine allowed me to start thinking—with you, Mark—about theater spaces, and how to play with and sometimes avoid the proscenium, to think about sets as all-encompassing and architectural. I learned a lot about how important space is to the experience of the language.

**MARK** There were so many problems—splinters, and people falling and being hurt. And Philip Littell, as Poseidon, wearing just a speedo the whole time ... I don't know how he did it.

**ASHER** The set for *Atlantis* seemed to be about the violence of perspective, about sickness and "the wound." *Atlantis* circulated around this idea of the authoritarian father, the incestual abusive father whom we all know and love—an American icon. We seem to have a familial, sexual attraction to his brutality and the power he has over us. We tried to permeate the environment with the smell of bodies, of bad cologne ... not Axe Body Spray exactly, but close. People recognized the smells. I was a little taken aback that people were like, "Is that semen?"

**TIM** The people in the steerage, the lower audience, got splashed on the face. But the actors looked up the balcony audience of "judges," who paid more for their seats, wore white wigs, and got served snacks ... that amuse-bouche of caramel dripped on Cheetos with crickets ...

**MARK** Asher, tell us about writing *Atlantis*.

**ASHER** Well, *Atlantis* was very weird. I started writing in a voice that felt sort of Irish, but not, kind of like baby talk, but not. Then it started to feel a bit like the *Katzenjammer Kids* comic strip, underscored by a very wet and nervous European immigrant's dread of renewed war. I also looked into the alt-right's adoption of Norse and Teutonic myths employed in Ariosophy, spiritual ideological systems based on Aryan-esoteric theories, such as Jörg Lanz von Liebenfels's *Theozoology and the Science of the Sodomite Apelings and the Divine Electron*—a racist, pseudoreligious, pseudoscientific diatribe against half-human, half-animal races breeding with German women. Liebenfels's interpretation of the Bible is of a sex manual. Words have coded meanings, so "water" or "wood" in the Bible mean sex. I think just about everything in the Bible, according to his interpretation, is sex.

**MARK** When was this published?

**ASHER** In the early twentieth century. Then I read the work of James Hillman, initiator of Archetypal psychology, which expanded my research into pre-Christian and Greek mythology. I'm acutely interested in our veneration of the unpredictable God-Father who tortures his children.

**TIM** You were saying earlier that *Sorry, Atlantis* is about your own parents' sex life ... ?

**ASHER** [*Laughter*] When I was a kid, during the women's movement in the '70s, the idea of "women's lib" was a joke. Men didn't know, and maybe still don't know, how to respond to ideas encompassed by the movement. It wouldn't be a revelation to say that men still struggle with masculinity. But one way they've responded, and this is part of Poseidon's character in *Atlantis*, has been to consume women, to devour them. I honestly don't want to imagine my parents' sex life. I think what I was really facing in the play was my own relation to gender as a child—to consuming adults, both male and female.

**TIM** In *Atlantis*, sexuality is definitely omnivorous. It's gay. It's straight. The play's everything.

**ASHER** Yes, but it would be unfortunate if the play were read only through the lens of gayness or queerness, or gender. Yes, there are gender upsets in my plays, and yes, sexuality is very funny. It can be sad and pathetic. It's kind of an engine. My characters are motivated by desire, whether for a ripe apple or a sexual experience. But all my plays are a kind of scraping attempt at liberation. Theater has the capacity to put the unconscious on display, especially parts of the cultural unconscious.

**TIM** "I am ... I said."

**ASHER** There's definitely something in Neil Diamond. Why was he such a figure in so many white middle-class kids' imaginations—or was it just in the Jewish kids' minds? He's the sensitive macho, the exotic (for the '60s) and safe mother's husband, the sexy not-dad, who could also be dad. I also love John Cassavetes's films from the '70s. The negotiation of masculinity in *Husbands*, for example, is urgent. And the misogyny is outrageous. *Atlantis* is steeped in misogyny, too. As are Greek myths, which inform American myths. The trial of the Menendez brothers in the '90s has all the components of a classical myth—parricide, wealth, intimations of too much intimacy between brothers, masculinity, power, revenge. Lyle and Erik Menendez are there in PoJo, the lizard twins.

**MARK** *Atlantis* also has Harry Who Tomato Face, that broken-down, damaged-male war hero of ancient myth.

**ASHER** He's based on a World War II vet who lived in my neighborhood, whose face was severely damaged. Of course, people feared and mocked him, and pitied him. Harry Who Tomato Face is a very powerful figure in the play. He's connected to the war trauma passed down in families from generation to generation. In Berkeley, where I spent a part of my childhood, there were many reminders of war, of struggle, of struggles lost.

**TIM** What about Freebird? She's the devil, right?

**ASHER** I wrote Freebird for Chelsea Rector. Chelsea is an amazing poet, with an incredible voice. However, unlike Chelsea, Freebird is the persona non grata that shows up whenever she likes, doesn't like anyone, prods and pokes everyone. Maybe she stands in for me? Maybe I take sadistic pleasure in verbal violence, crassness, saying what no one wants you to say? In eliciting fear, even …

**TIM** Why is theater a good place to bring fear?

**ASHER** To discharge it. Theater's always had a role in hosting the parade of uglies—not necessarily the ills in domestic life, but those of political life. The play is like a carcass. Actors pull the carcass apart and allow us to look at its components. As an audience member, you're sort of captive. You're often presented with what you *don't* want to feel. You may come to the theater expecting something important to unfold before you, as well you should, but those expectations are material for the actors, for the play itself. In a lot of contemporary theater and performance, we

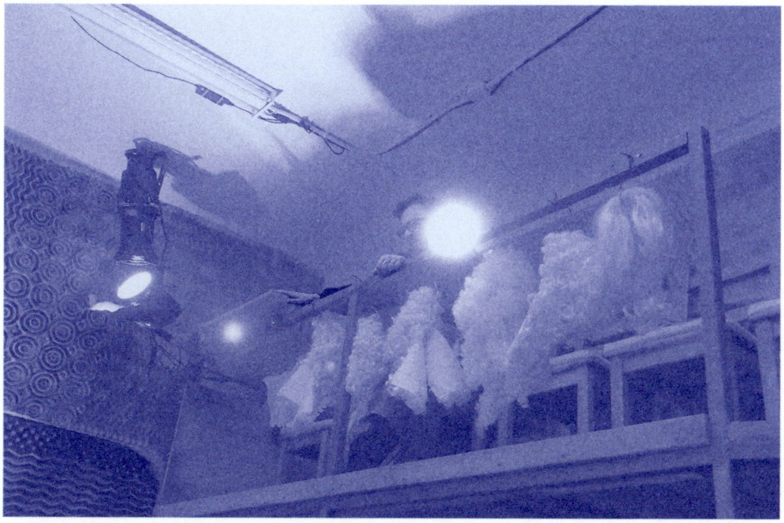

Rehearsal view, Asher Hartman in judges' balcony, set of *Sorry, Atlantis: Eden's Achin' Organ Seeks Revenge*, Machine Project, Los Angeles, 2017

watch each other watching, thinking. We watch reactions, feelings of complicity, disagreement, boredom, anxiety, assent.

**MARK** For me, your plays are the hyper-experience of too much information. In terms of feeling and sensation, they're ecstatic. I've watched them performed again and again because I want a different kind of experience, to feel things in my body in a way that is not ... resolved, somatically or emotionally. I connect strongly to your work because it's antiteleological, versus, say, a play where a person is allowed only the one self, and the story is just that self's transformation into a new self, a new solid state.

**ASHER** Yes. I may not understand the Latin Mass, but I know the English version is not good. I use language as a kind of invocation, and I feel your same dissatisfaction with the concept of transformation, and personal victory. Really good actors spend a tremendous amount of time trying to bend the language into human action and psychology, which then opens up feeling that can't be understood logically. The Gawdafful actors make known what is real on the street—that tragic, bitter laughter of someone who has lost everything. These plays aren't polemics. This is not didactic theater, which usually amounts to "We all agree, don't we?" I think of these plays as collective works performed by a certain group of people, at a certain time, dependent on the intricacies of their relationships and intimate understandings of American sensibilities that roil around in seemingly ornate and crusty language.

**TIM** Do you think any of these plays will be staged again, by someone else?

**ASHER** I can't even ... that's such a funny question. My fear is that they would be restaged with declamatory passion, or gleeful adherence to ideals of Absurdist or Surrealist aesthetics. America, as a concept, is already painfully absurd. A Cheeto, for example, a Chicken Screamer, a "fully loaded" burrito—these need no garland, no added seriousness or art. These are indexes of uncertainty wed to capital, wed to the body, consumed and shat out to repurpose yet another day of living, which we love to call hope but which may also be an end.

The artist Mark Allen produced *Purple Electric Play (PEP!)*, *Mr. Akita*, and *Sorry, Atlantis: Eden's Achin' Organ Seeks Revenge* at Machine Project, Los Angeles, an art space he founded and directed from 2003–18.

Tim Reid is a playwright and performer who joined Asher Hartman's Gawdafful National Theater as the assistant director of *Sorry, Atlantis*.

***Purple Electric Play (PEP!)***
Machine Project, Los Angeles, 2014

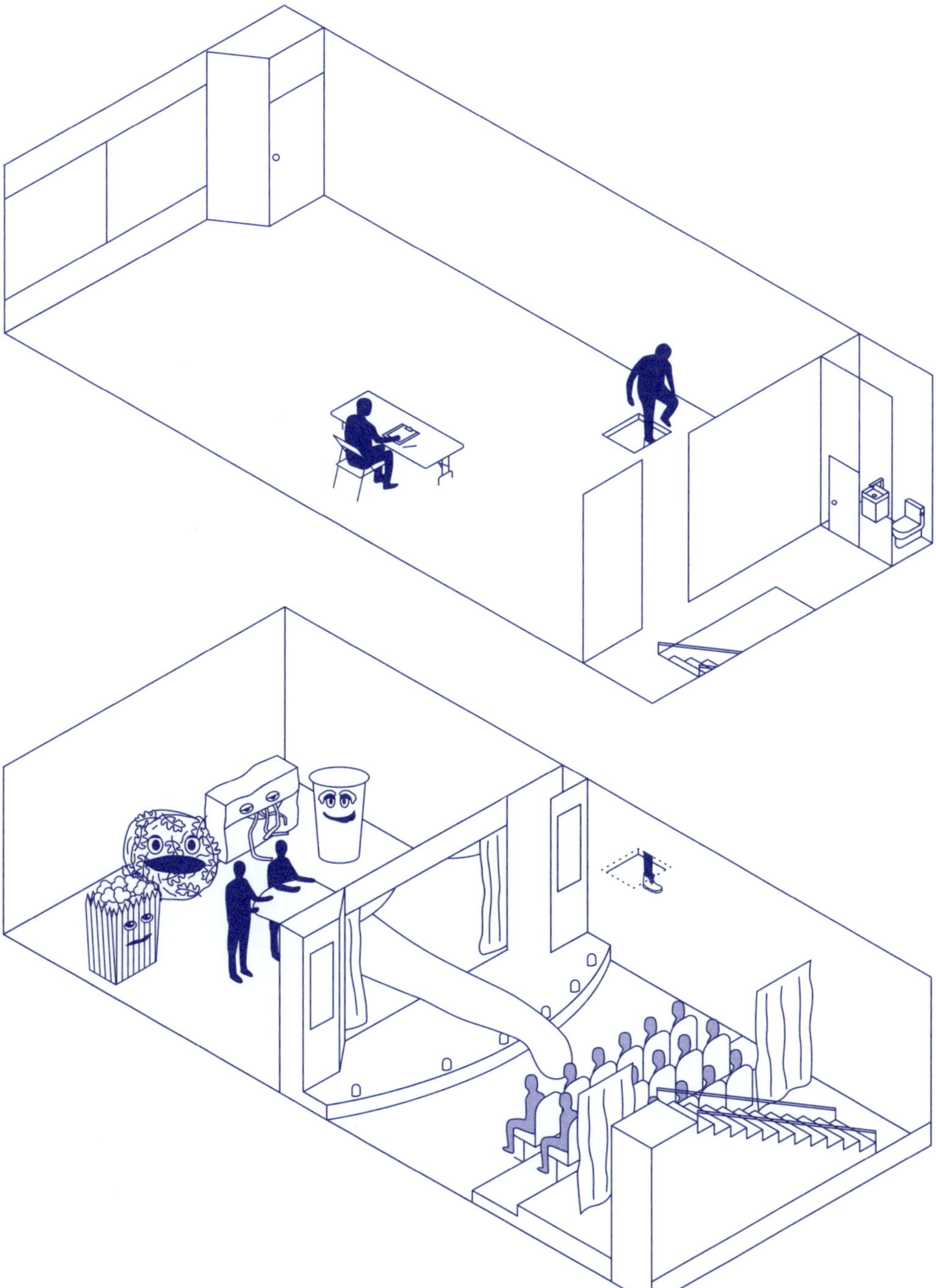

**Mr. Akita**

Tang Teaching Museum, Skidmore College, Saratoga Springs, New York, in the exhibition *Machine Project: The Platinum Collection (live by special request)*, 2015

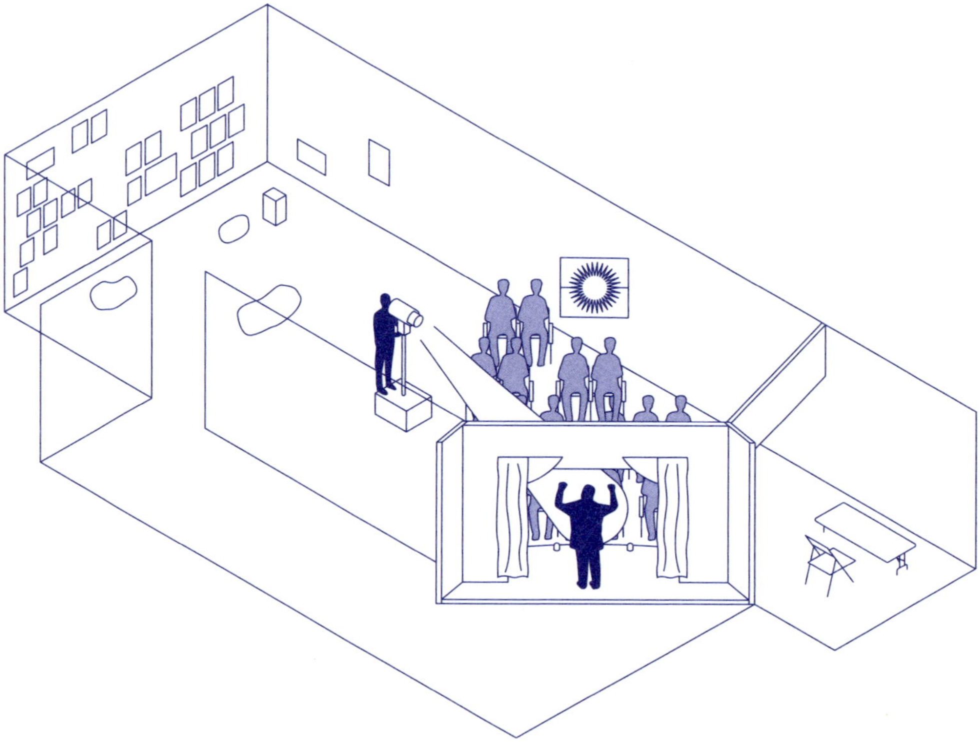

***Sorry, Atlantis: Eden's Achin' Organ Seeks Revenge***

Machine Project, Los Angeles, 2017

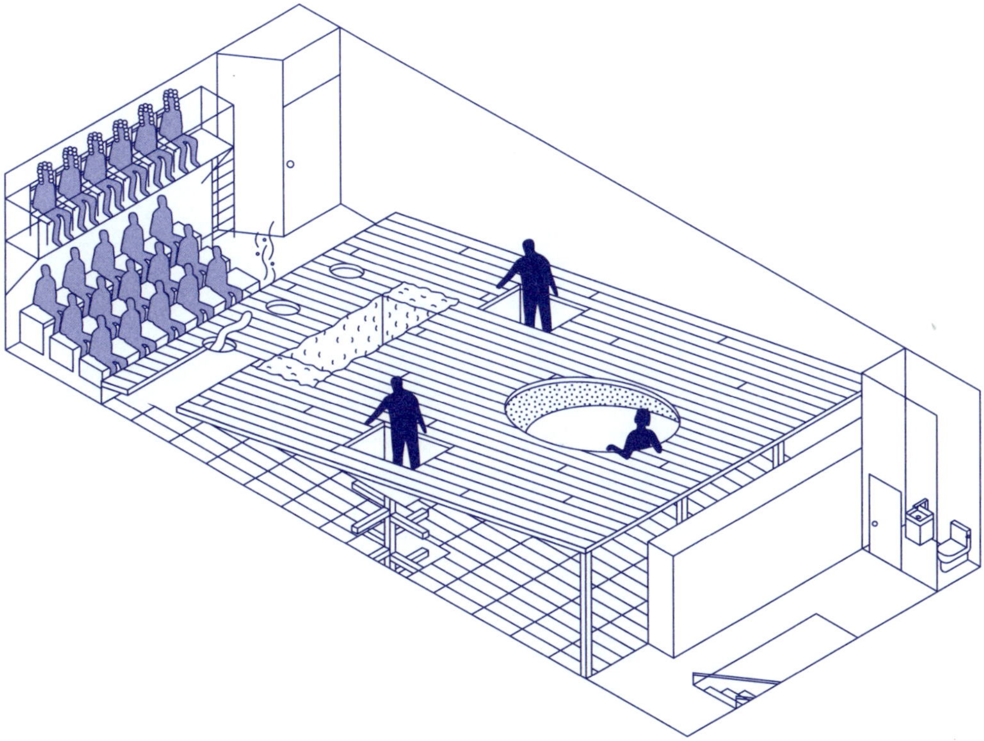

# Photography Credits

**SINGLE-COLOR IMAGES**

p. 8, Cliff Hengst, backstage at Machine Project, Los Angeles, 2015, Photo by Ian Byers-Gamber / p. 10, Performance view, Charles Nelson Reilly (Joe Seely) in *The All Stars of Non Violet Communication*, LACE, Los Angeles, 2011, Photo by Takahiro Yamamoto / pp.14 and 16, Photos by Marianne Williams / p. 20, Performance view, Star (Philip Littell) in *Purple Electric Play (PEP!)*, Machine Project, 2014, Photo by Marianne Williams / pp. 23 and 26, Photos by Marianne Williams / pp. 28–29, Performance view, Vital Organ (Jasmine Orpilla, left) and Vital Organ II (Kalean Ung, right) in *Purple Electric Play*, Photo by Marianne Williams / pp. 68–69, Rehearsal view, Man (Cliff Hengst) in *Mr. Akita*, Tang Teaching Museum, Skidmore College, Saratoga Springs, New York, 2015, Photo by Ian Byers-Gamber / pp. 86–87, Rehearsal view, Po (Paul Outlaw) in *Sorry, Atlantis: Eden's Achin' Organ Seeks Revenge*, Machine Project, 2017, Photo by Ian Byers-Gamber / p. 128, Performance view, Vital Organ in *Purple Electric Play*, Photo by Marianne Williams / p. 145, Performance view, Po and Jo (Joe Seely) in *Sorry, Atlantis*, Photo by Ian Byers-Gamber / pp. 146–47, Rehearsal view, *Purple Electric Play*; front row, from left: Asher Hartman and Philip Littell; third row, from left: Carol Guidry (choreographer) and Zut Alors, Photo by Marianne Williams / p. 148, Judges' balcony and lower seating for rabble, set of *Sorry, Atlantis*, Photo by Gema Galian / p. 150, Photo by Ian Byers-Gamber / p. 155, Photos courtesy Machine Project / p. 156, Photos by Marianne Williams / p. 159, above: Photo by Gema Galian; below: Photo by Haruko Tanaka / p. 163, Photo by Haruko Tanaka / p. 170, Performance view, Large Floppy Arm With Yellow Quill Pen in *Purple Electric Play*, Photo by Marianne Williams / p. 172, Rehearsal view, Jo in *Sorry, Atlantis*, Photo by Ian Byers-Gamber

**FULL-COLOR IMAGES**

Performance views, *Purple Electric Play (PEP!)*, Machine Project, 2014, Photos by Marianne Williams: p. 129, background: Audience (Joe Seely); upper inset: Star (Philip Littell); lower inset: Audience / p. 130, background, from left: Audience, Vital Organ (Jasmine Orpilla), and Star; inset, from left: Vital Organ, White Afro, Zen Monk, and Vital Organ II (Kalean Ung) / p. 131, upper left: Vital Organs, Audience, and Tooth; upper right: Audience; middle right: Star and Vital Organs; bottom, from left: Lo-Phat, Donkey, Paper Horse, Starvation, and Salad Bar / pp. 132–33, background: Donkey, Lo-Phat, Vital Organ, Star, Starvation, and Salad Bar; inset: Mad Shadow (Chelsea Rector) / p. 134, background: Vital Organ; upper inset: Vital Organs and Donkey; lower inset: Mother Theater's Tongue / p. 135, upper inset: Donkey, Pizza Box, and

Unless otherwise noted, all images courtesy Gawdafful National Theater

Starvation; middle insets: Audience, Vital Organ, Songbird (Drew Thataussie), and Star; bottom inset: Vital Organs, Star, and Audience

Performance views, *Mr. Akita*, Tang Teaching Museum, Skidmore College, 2015, Photos by Ian Byers-Gamber: pp. 136–39, Man (Cliff Hengst) and *Sun Burn (Split) 1* (2012) by Emily Joyce

Performance views, *Sorry, Atlantis: Eden's Achin' Organ Seeks Revenge*, Machine Project, 2017: pp. 140–41, background: Poseidon (Philip Littell), Photo by Gema Galian; upper right insets: Sledgeweed (Zut Lorz), Photos by Ian Byers-Gamber; bottom inset, from left: Jo (Joe Seely) and Peaseashit, Photo by Gema Galian / p. 142, upper left: Sledgeweed, Photo by Ian Byers-Gamber; middle: Jo (left foreground), Po (Paul Outlaw, right foreground), and Sledgeweed (distance), Photo by Haruko Tanaka; bottom: Harry Who Tomato Face (Michael Bonnabel, foreground), Photo by Gema Galian; upper right: Poseidon and Harry Who Tomato Face, Photo by Haruko Tanaka / p. 143, above, background: Freebird (Chelsea Rector, left foreground), Foul Puppet Bird (right foreground), Sledgeweed, and Poseidon, Photo by Haruko Tanaka; above, inset: Sledgeweed and Poseidon (distance) and PoJo (foreground), Photo by Ian Byers-Gamber; lower left: Poseidon, Harry Who Tomato Face, and PoJo, Photo by Ian Byers-Gamber; lower right: Po and Hairy Hairy Woman (Philip Littell), Photo by Ian Byers-Gamber / p. 144, above: Jo, Photo by Ian Byers-Gamber; lower left: Freebird (foreground), Photo by Gema Galian; lower right: Po, Photo by Ian Byers-Gamber

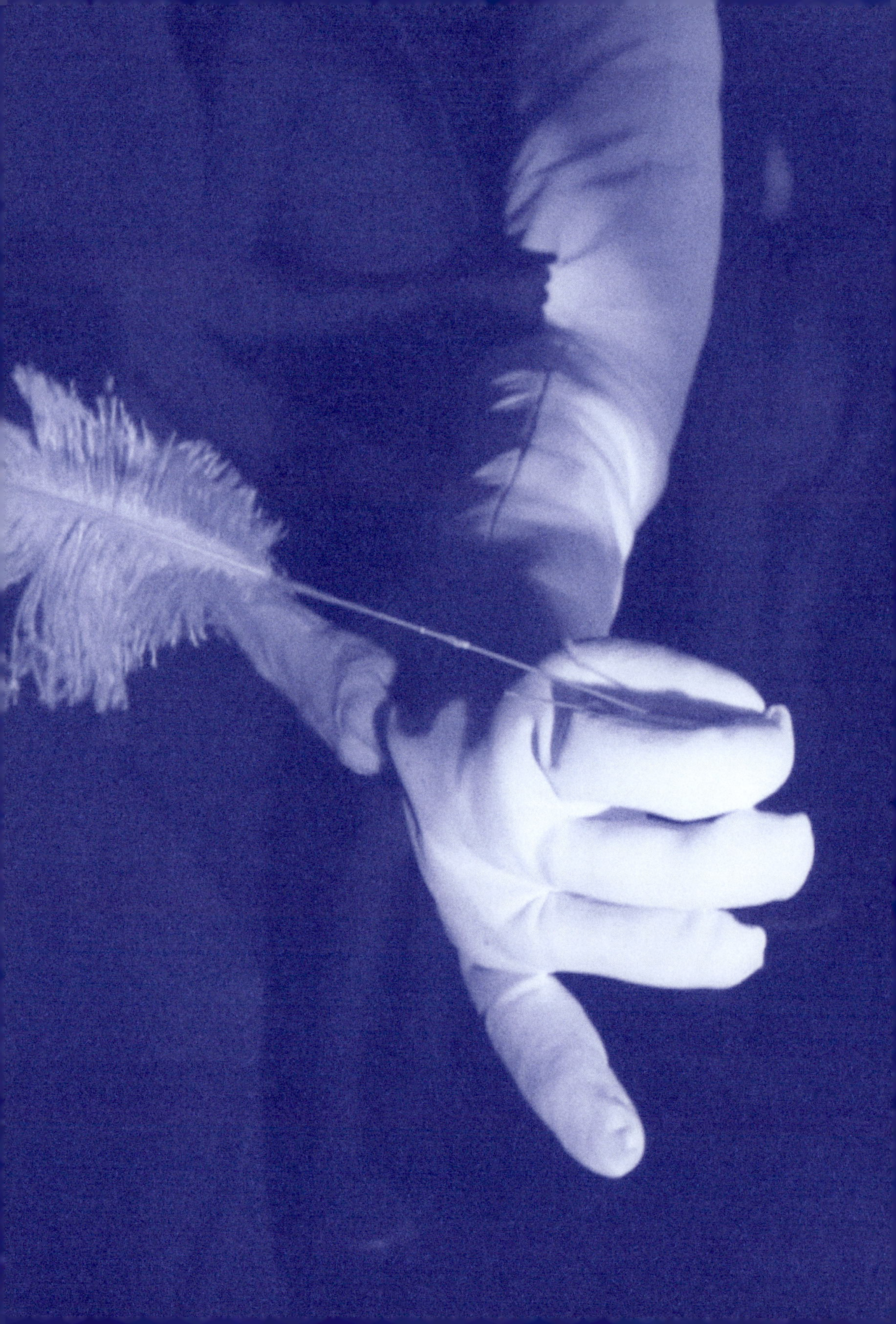

# About Asher Hartman

Asher Hartman is an interdisciplinary artist, writer, director, and intuitive practitioner whose work at the junction of visual art and theater centers on the exploration of the self in relation to western histories and ideologies. His theatrical performances are particularly concerned with psychological violence in American culture. Much of his practice developed at Machine Project, Los Angeles, between 2010 and 2017.

In collaboration with the Gawdafful National Theater, founded in 2010, Hartman has written and directed *Bad Thing* (2010, Sea and Space Explorations, Los Angeles), *Annie Okay* (2010, Hammer Museum, Los Angeles, with Machine Project), *The All Stars of Non Violet Communication* (2011, Human Resources, LACE, and Highways Performance Space, Los Angeles), *See What Love the Father Has Given Us* (2012, Machine Project), *Glass Bang* (2013, MAK Center for Art and Architecture at Rudolph M. Schindler's Fitzpatrick-Leland House, Los Angeles, as part of Machine Project's engagement in the Getty Foundation's *Pacific Standard Time Presents: Modern Architecture in L.A.*, also with Cannonball, Miami, and Southern Exposure, San Francisco), *Purple Electric Play (PEP!)* (2014, Machine Project), *Mr. Akita* (2015, Tang Teaching Museum, Skidmore College, Saratoga Springs, New York, as part of the exhibition *Machine Project: The Platinum Collection (live by special request)*; 2017, University of California, Berkeley Art Museum & Pacific Film Archive; 2017, Hauser & Wirth, Los Angeles), *The Silver, the Black, the Wicked Dance* (2016, Los Angeles County Museum of Art [LACMA]), *Sorry, Atlantis: Eden's Achin' Organ Seeks Revenge* (2017, Machine Project), *The Lost Privilege Company* (2018, USC Visions and Voices series and Pieter Performance Space, Los Angeles), and *The Dope Elf* (2019, Yale Union, Portland, Oregon; 2020, The Lab, San Francisco).

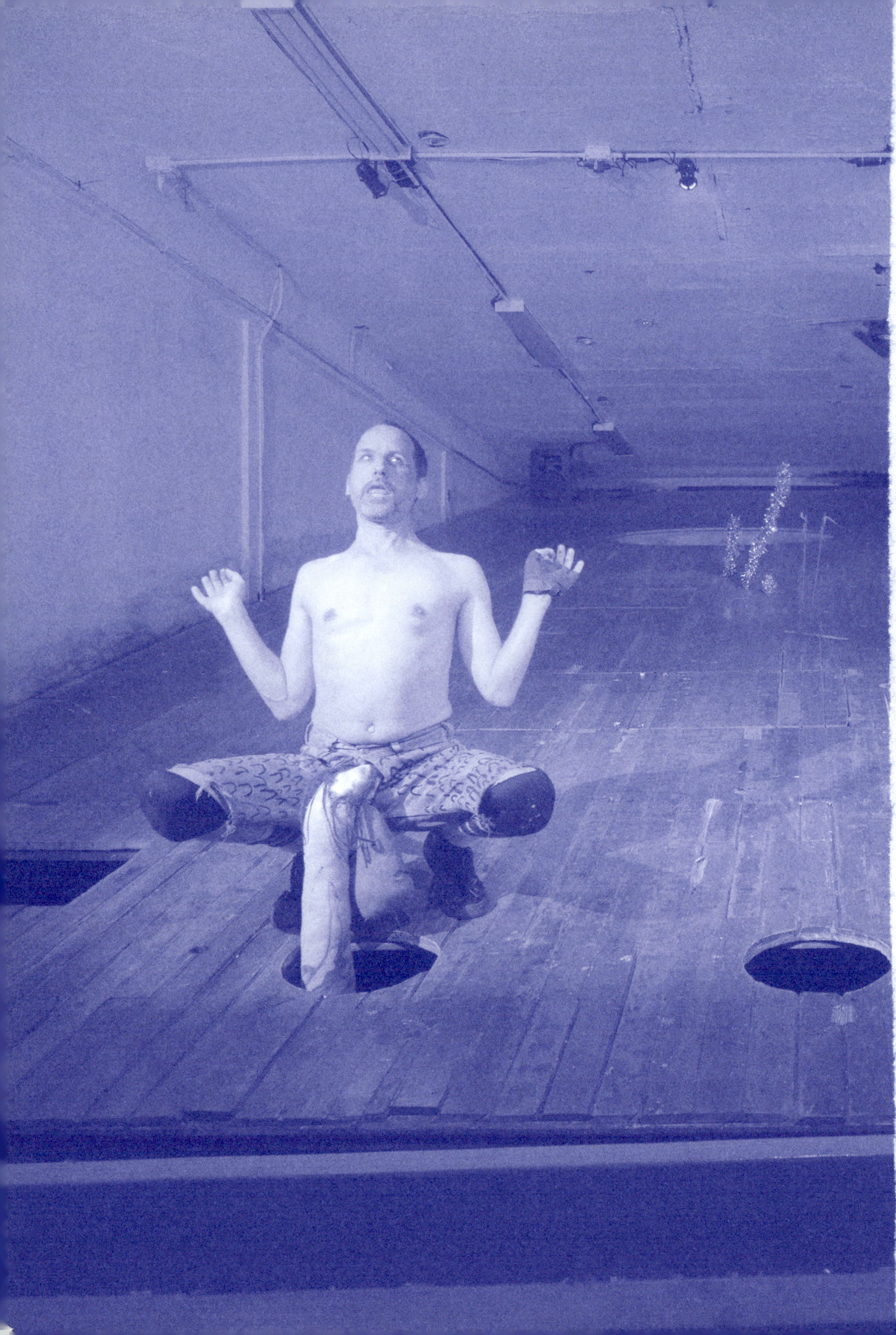